Endorsements

Shari's loving and giving heart is evident to anyone around her. She truly is a woman who uses her platform to make a difference in the lives of women in need of compassion, grace, and forgiveness. She is vulnerable enough to use her own past pain to prevent the future pain of others.

PASTOR CAROLINE BARNETT
The Dream Center and author of *Willing to Walk on Water*

An incredibly insightful and transparent story about some of life's most critical issues. Shari was brave to tell us her story and we can all learn and benefit from it. Her ongoing ministry, and now this excellent book, will continue to help a lot of people—and steer others from unnecessary pain and anguish.

TOM GEHRING
Lawyer and author of *Settle It! …and be Blessed*

Shari Rigby is a woman of God, full of integrity, beauty, and grace. Her story captured within these pages reads like a romance novel only God could write. I could not put it down. I had to know what happened next. I had to know how she went from the little girl on the run to God's leading lady, the woman that I know today! Love you, sister. You are brave and beautiful and will give many people a voice to tell their stories of romance…a romance novel only God could write.

EDEE BURCH
Regional Manager, California, K-Love and Air1

It is not by mistake that Shari Rigby was sent to me to transform her into the beautiful, flawess talent she is today. Her miraculous story is life changing and her n every performance we create!

JHN KIRBY
Acting Coach

As a former director for a Crisis Pregnancy Center and having a master's degree in biblical counseling, I worked with women of all ages in their journeys and decision making in their often-times unwanted pregnancies. This is a very insightful and candid look into the life of a very beautiful and talented lady, and it stands as an inspiration for all girls and women to draw upon. Truly through Christ we are able to be new creatures (2 Corinthians 5:17). I highly recommend this easy-to-read book for women of all ages.

SHANNON SLOANE, M.A.

There are lot of books out there where people tell their stories. But I feel that this one is indeed special because no stone was left unturned. Shari shares her most vulnerable and even ugly moments with the reader as if we are right there with her. We cry with her, we cheer for her, and we see God's healing hands in her life.

KERRI POMAROLLI
Comedian on *The Tonight Show*, ABC, NBC, Comedy Central
Author of *Guys Like Girls Named Jennie* and *Moms' Night Out Devotional*

Beautifully Flawed is an amazing true story of God's amazing grace and redeeming love. Shari's testimony and story take the reader along a journey of life where readers will be able to identify many facets of their life. This descriptive journey is a page turner to the end, and ultimately points to Jesus. Despite the trials and tribulations that we face, we have confidence in this: Jesus is the author and finisher of our faith…and He, who began a good work in all of us will bring it to completion. His grace is sufficient for you, and His power is made perfect in your weakness. Enjoy!

ANNE NEILSON
Artist and gallery owner
Author of *Angels in Our Midst* and *Strokes of Compassion*

Peace. That's what I felt when I first met Shari on the *October Baby* set. It's what I continue to experience whenever I'm around her. Shari is openly loving, greatly compassionate, and at times, courageously vulnerable—all of which you'll find when reading her book. It's no surprise that she has an affinity for Wonder Woman. Shari is she.

JASON BURKEY
Actor, *October Baby* and *Mom's Night Out*

I am so thankful that Shari is willing to tell her story. It is one of second chances, redemption, and renewal, reminding us that God can take our brokenness and do amazing things.

J. W. CLARKE
Director of Program, Billy Graham Evangelistic Association

In the captivating autobiography *Beautifully Flawed*, Shari Rigby unabashedly bares her soul and lays out her life before us with candid—and at times unsettling—transparency, selflessly casting aside concern over the reader's judgment or shock. Shari exposes her life experience so that others will benefit by believing how powerfully God can transform a life—exiting the former darkness and entering into the radiance of being a new creation in Christ who exists only for the purposes and glory of God. *Beautifully Flawed* is a message of grace, hope, and redemption that will endure as an example that God can take any life and make something of great brilliance and beauty out of dire brokenness.

SUZANNE NILES
The Salvation Army Vision Network, SAVNtv

I truly cannot even begin to express what this beautiful lady and true kindred spirit has meant to my faith, my career, and my life. Our friendship has blessed and encouraged me beyond words and helped strengthen me to become the more capable woman that I am today. I am so incredibly thankful that she has chosen to tell her story in this way. It is a precious gift when someone allows you to see the world through their eyes and invites you to join them on their journey. Walk with her a little while and let her story breathe life into yours.

COLLEEN TRUSLER
Actress, *October Baby*

From the women of The Dream Center and Ida Somero, Dream Center Foundation, Executive Director:

> *Beautifully Flawed* is a dramatic narrative life story about a young woman faced with poor decisions, self-destructive behavior, and the negative consequences. The story ends as a redemptive account of what the Lord can do if you trust and follow His leading.

> An emotionally enthralling story of trading in heartache, pain, and self-loathing for the redemptive beauty only God can provide.

> Any young lady dreaming about living the elusive perfect life should read *Beautifully Flawed*. The truth about the destructive consequences of using sex to attract love is a powerful message woven throughout every page.

> Painting poignant scenes of raw and relatable emotion, any woman can empathize with Shari's harrowing journey of young adulthood and finding her true identity in Christ. A compelling and encouraging read!

> Set free from the mask and fairy-tale of performance and having to face the reality and pain of her life, Shari learns that God's grace was indeed sufficient for her! An encouragement to any woman traveling down a "broken road."

> After seeking acceptance in all the wrong places, Shari finally faces the shocking truth of her past. After exposing a shameful secret sin, physical pain, disappointment, and rejection, God brought her to a place of submission and repentance. She was made to tear down idols and submit to God's will while discovering what true beauty is!

beautifully
FLAWED

BroadStreet
PUBLISHING

These are my (the author's) memories
and I am telling my life story as I remember it.
To protect the privacy of others,
some names have been changed.

Published by BroadStreet Publishing Group
Racine, Wisconsin, USA
www.broadstreetpublishing.com

Beautifully Flawed: Finding Your Radiance in the Imperfections of Your Life
By Shari Rigby with Claire Yorita Lee

ISBN: 978-1-4245-4983-2 (paperback)
ISBN: 978-1-4245-5009-8 (e-book)

All Scripture is from the New American Standard Bible, Copyright © 1960, 1962, 1963, 1968, 1971, 1972, 1973, 1975, 1977, 1995 by The Lockman Foundation. Used by permission.

Cover photography: Mario Barberio
Cover design: Rachel Hendrix
Typesetting: Katherine Lloyd

Stock or custom editions of BroadStreet Publishing titles may be purchased in bulk for educational, business, ministry, fundraising, or sales promotional use. For information, please e-mail info@broadstreetpublishing.com.

Printed in the United States of America

15 16 17 18 19 20   7 6 5 4 3 2 1

Dedication

First, this story belongs to my Savior, who gave me life. Who chose me for such a time as this to use my life's journey to serve Him. He has turned my ashes to garland and removed the smell of smoke from my body. I will serve Him all my days!

Matthew, my gift from God. You love me like a queen. You are truly a man of integrity, character, and beauty. You are my rock star! I am so grateful that you and I get to do life together. You love me with all my flaws and continue to see the beauty in me even when I'm a mess. I love being your *wife*.

My sons. Donnie and Levi, you always inspire me. I am so blessed to have been given the gift to see you both grow up. You are both my heroes. I love you!

Ray and Sharon Rigby, my incredible parents. Dad and Mom, to this day you still share the sweet stories of my childhood with me. Mom, every time you grab my hand, hold it tight, look into my eyes, and share with me about my birth and the moment my dad first laid eyes on me in the hospital, your sweet face shines like it's your first time telling me the story. Then you continue with the fun stories about me and my childhood antics, and before I know it, Dad joins in with a smile, shaking his head, and adding to the story by telling me about my big brother, saying I looked like a little baby chick and that's how I got my nickname, *Chickie*.

All of this to say, no matter what I did or didn't do as a child, a young woman, or an adult, your love for me is overwhelming, bigger and deeper than I will ever know. There is no way that I can ever repay you both for standing by me during my foolish days as a youth. You gave Donnie and me a place to live, money to help us survive, and most important, the security of a home to Donnie when I couldn't provide one.

Mom and Dad, thank you for staying the course with me and reminding me that *I am special*. No matter what I do in life, no matter what I achieve or don't, you both love me and call me *daughter*.

Contents

Foreword

I've always been a strong person, at least that's what my chiropractor tells me every time he finishes adjusting this or that. "Something about you Hendrix kids...you were born strong," he says. I am thankful for that strength—for endurance in the valleys, for the powerhouse our bodies can be to get us up the mountain again.

Perhaps I'm assuming too much here, but I believe every single person on this earth has been impacted by a woman whose strength and agility are coupled with grace and gentleness. There is something otherworldly that happens when we encounter these types of women. They simply have the power to change the atmosphere. I've also come to realize that this is the very picture of Shari Rigby. Grace is her heartbeat. Gentleness is the fruit on her breakfast table. Love is the blood in her veins. Knowing her has actually made me more beautiful, and who doesn't want a little more beautiful?

With this gratitude I am often reminded of how particularly fragile we are—how physical beauty may fade but the nature of our heart matters all the more; how frail the mere body is capable of becoming when stripped of His original design; how easily our hearts can break when we feel like we don't matter, like we've drawn the short straw and no one cares. As I read through Shari's story, I couldn't help but feel her pain through the words on the paper. I wanted to holler out, "I know exactly why you did that!" I also wanted to give her lots of hugs, look her in the eye and say how sorry I was that all those bad things happened.

Wounds lead to bodies that bare their marks. Wounds can

also lead to hearts surrounded by electrified, barbed-wire fences if we let them fester and never walk through healing. After all the piercing arrows, all the years of wondering where her heart would find security, the spirit of the living God met her in all her messy glory and whispered gently of His marvelous plan. Shari did what any good actor would—she listened and she responded.

I like to think my inner strength and dependence on God has sustained me through my life, not just my ability to bend and not break, even though my brokenness is made perfect in Him. Strength is a part of my story, the details that will one day complete the tapestry He's weaving.

Story is power, and we all have one. Every single one of us. You are often tempted to believe yours is obsolete, but let me tell you that it's not just *a* story, it's *your* story. It's perfectly flawed and full of grace. Existing in the present as a timeless memoir, it is continually being written through the ebbs and flows while constantly changing like the seasons—expanding and contracting as the breath that spoke life into you.

The written story shakes generations and moves people to change. It also has the ability to empower the converse—our indifference to the lie that we live surrounded by invalid details. Shari walks the reader through her story with ease and victory. The more you read the more you realize that these tiny details of our lives do matter. They shape our story into a masterpiece. Our seemingly broken and messy lives belong to the one who holds us in His hands.

Through a series of events you have found *Beautifully Flawed* in your hands today. Like Shari, whose story gives life to these pages like marrow to dry bones, you have a story to tell. Let hers inspire you.

—Rachel Hendrix,
Actress from *October Baby*

Introduction

Life's journey is *beautifully flawed.*

This morning I am sitting here, drinking my hot coffee full of yummy vanilla creamer, thinking about all the things that I want to share with you before you begin reading *Beautifully Flawed.* My story...my life laid out before you. I think *Why my story?* All I can think of is that I said yes to sharing it. I said yes to the Lord ten years ago when I was told to get out of the boat and start walking, so I jumped. And here we are, you and me, getting ready to take a journey together through the pages of my book.

I loved growing up in a small town in North Dakota. It gave way to days full of playing outside for hours, roaming the little town on my bike to catch maybe a few minutes of conversation with a neighbor, or ending up in the little movie theater that sat in the middle of town with my eyes glued to the big screen. But whatever my day looked like, I would dream of having a fairy-tale life. I would dream of becoming the *leading lady,* seeing only the beautiful starlets on screen.

I started school and I realized very quickly that I wasn't the perfect one. This was tough for me, being the little girl with a thick frame. I had never seen myself as anything but perfect until the day when I realized that I was seeking out love and acceptance from others. It seemed like validation from the opposite sex was my boast, my way to being the *leading lady* that I longed to be. My identity was slipping further and further away.

As the years passed, the roller coaster of life continued on the winding journey that seemed like it was never going to stop. Up and down through the valleys of darkness to a small hill with a light shining just beyond the horizon, but it seemed like I just couldn't get there. Getting on my knees and crying out to the Lord, asking Him to open the doors to change in my life. Giving up this false idea of who I wanted to be, and who I thought I should be, brought a new gift. A gift that led the way to my truly becoming the *leading lady*. Leading me to freedom and on to fulfilling my lifelong dream. To finding love that is greater than I could have ever asked for. I believe that the Lord wants each and every one of us to receive this freedom and to know that nothing can separate us from His love.

I believe everyone has a story, a powerful life message to share with others, to give hope and to help us remember we are not alone. Our life situations and relationships shape us, building our character while facing trials and tribulations, but also celebrating the goodness of God's grace. I believe God has called me "for such a time as this" to encourage men and women of all ages to appreciate their flaws, to see themselves as beautiful, to use their past experiences and not to be held captive by them. I want you to be the confident, spirit-filled warrior that God created you to be. You too have been called for such a time as this.

I still get lost sometimes, but the difference now is that I know who I am. My identity lies in someone so much greater than I am, in a Savior who loves me. That speaks to me and reminds me that the only approval I need is from Him, not man. I am called lovely, beautiful, and gifted. And each day I die to myself in order to become what I was purposefully created for, giving Him control so that I can do what it is He has called me to do.

My hope is that as you read my story, you will see that we have all been given certain talents and gifts, and a passion that runs deep in our hearts to fulfill a calling. Each and every one of us has value, and God has made us special and with purpose. Life will be full of challenges, but it's how we use those challenges that make a difference and helps make us.

My journey hasn't always been a pretty one, but I have found the beauty in it. I pray that as you read about my life, the challenges, the loves, the mistakes, you might be inspired to open up and share about yours. Hopefully then you too will understand and appreciate that we are all beautifully flawed.

Blessings,
Shari

Part One
LIGHTS, CAMERA, ACTION
Losing Myself

n the middle of town sat an old movie theater, one of my favorite places to spend an afternoon. It stole my heart with its towering screen and plush velvet seats, as the smell of popcorn wafted in from the lobby. I was content to sit there for hours, imagining myself as the characters I watched sing, dance, and fall in love. I could be anyone I wanted—a superhero, a queen, or an undercover cop. The possibilities were infinite.

I found musicals especially enticing, watching the young man sing his heart out to the beautiful starlet. I remember standing in line with my mom one day, waiting to buy tickets to *Grease*, staring at the poster of the beautiful blonde and the handsome, raven-haired rebel. When the lights went out and the movie shined up onto the big screen, I had stars in my eyes. Afterward, all I could think about was wearing black satin pants, a leather jacket, and red lipstick, smoking a cigarette while my dream man sang to me.

Many years later I continued to cling to the dream I so desperately desired. Living in a fantasy world of who I could be and not who I really was, I related every new movie and every new song to my life. I longed to be the starlet, to look like a supermodel, and to be with the rebellious rock star. I wanted to be the *leading lady* I had seen on the screen, no matter what the cost. Even if it meant *losing myself.*

1

Innocence Lost

>

"Trust takes years to build,
seconds to break and forever to repair."
HARRIET MORGAN

Standing next to my mom's car, with tears and dirt running down my face, I was shaking and emotionally exhausted. My bottom hurt very badly. When I looked down and saw blood, I got really scared. I knew my mom was upset because she had been driving all over town looking for me. I was dying inside, feeling dirty and ashamed, like it was all my fault. My mother's eyes were angry, and she kept saying how she was so worried about me and how I had scared her half to death. I needed to think quick. I didn't want her to know what had just happened. Think, think... I just kept crying. Then I pointed to my bottom, and the words just came out of my mouth. "I was riding home on my bike and I fell on the middle bar." She could see the blood on my shorts, and her eyes went from anger to concern in a second. I had lied and gotten away with it. She would never know the truth.

Cooperstown was a great place to spend my youngest years. It was a sweet town of about a thousand people, a pin dot between Bismarck, Fargo, and Grand Forks. Cooperstown was lush and green, with trees surrounding the perimeter. In fact, the forest was one of the safest places for me to be…at least I thought so. I could lose myself in them for hours and never feel lost. The trees provided the most incredible scenic landscape for hours of play.

My parents had built a home on the outskirts of town, so we could see the massive tree line from both the front yard and back porch. Running through the trees, I got lost in my dreams of cowboys and Indians. I grew up watching *Gunsmoke*, *True Grit*, *The Good, the Bad and the Ugly*, *Baretta*, *Police Woman*, and many more. My dad loved Westerns and cop shows; therefore, so did I. I could spend hours using my imagination, taking on the bad guys and saving the world.

My dad was the sheriff of this little town. In fact, I remember watching *Dirty Harry* and thinking my dad looked a lot like him. He would put on the police uniform and transform into someone else. He seemed to love his job and the people he worked with.

I don't remember spending much time with my dad growing up. He was a silent warrior who enjoyed serving his people. The local courthouse was my dad's office, and if you pulled up to the side of the building, you would see the small entry door to the police headquarters. Attached to it were several old jail cells, so everything took place in one building under one roof. The police would arrest you, take you to their headquarters, and throw you in jail until you went before a judge in the upstairs courthouse.

I visited the courthouse whenever I could. I would roll up on my bike, drop it in the grass, and run to see my dad. Most of the time he was busy, so I made my way to the dark, smelly, old jail cells, sneaking around, hoping to see the kitty that was always having babies down there. Before I knew it, I was lying on the cold concrete floor with the kitties, holding them and dreaming my mom and dad might let me have one to take home. Unfortunately, by the time my parents found me, I would be having an allergic reaction to those kittens. Unable to see or breathe and feeling itchy all over, I didn't care. I just loved being with them.

My mom was often compared to Elizabeth Taylor, with her long black hair and striking features. She never saw herself as a beauty, though, always thinking she wasn't pretty enough. My mom and I spent a lot of time alone since my dad was always at the courthouse or working side jobs to make extra money.

Our home was a happy place, with green shag carpet upstairs and blue shag carpet downstairs. It was the '70s, so if you had shag carpeting and a new house in Cooperstown, that meant you were doing well. My room was green and yellow, full of Barbies and dolls my mom and grandma had made, with pretty faces, dark hair like theirs, and handcrafted dresses. I spent hours playing with my dolls, giving them haircuts and creating new looks for them while daydreaming of my Ken-doll husband. Sometimes my brother, Randy, who was five years older and a teaser, would come in with a smile and ask to play. Of course I said yes, and for a brief minute he played nicely with a doll before ripping its head off, throwing it at me, and running off, with me trailing behind in tears.

I was a dreamer for sure and always seemed to live in a world of make-believe. I loved pretending to be Wonder Woman with a crystal jet that could fly anywhere. My "crystal jet" was my two-wheel bike, and it took me all over Cooperstown. I was unstoppable, a free spirit...and my mother knew it. She didn't like that I would just take off, so she took me out in the morning, sat me on the back porch with all my Barbie dolls, and told me, "Play here and don't leave." But the moment she went inside, I ran down the porch stairs, jumped on my bike, and took off down the street, never looking back.

I rode through town, taking it all in. My first stop was the little grocery store to grab some bubble gum. Then I made my way to the nearby restaurant just to catch a whiff of the warm comfort food cooking in the back kitchen. Finally, I arrived at the movie theatre in the middle of town. Walking in, I smelled fresh popcorn mixed with mold from the melting snow before heading into the small, dark movie theatre. Deep emotion hit the pit of my stomach every time I sat down in one of the creaky old seats. I could sit there for hours, losing myself in movies, dreaming of who I could be. Mesmerized by the perfect leading lady on screen, I was drawn to her beauty and character, wishing I could be her rather than the flawed little girl I saw myself as.

Of course my mom eventually found me, and she lectured me all the way home about the dangers of wandering the streets alone, while I walked my bike alongside her, daydreaming and not really hearing a word she said. I always seemed to come up with some little white lie to tell her that would ease her frustration with me.

My mom introduced my brother and me to Jesus at a very young age. We attended a Lutheran church where I enjoyed Sunday school, hearing Bible stories and eating the star-shaped grape-jelly-on-white-bread sandwiches. My mother was a Sunday school teacher, so we were there every week and I helped her get the craft activity together for class. I loved helping and acting like I was a teacher too.

My first acting gig was at this little church. It was Christmas, and I landed the lead role of Mary, mother of baby Jesus. I was so proud sitting there in my classic white felt gown and baby-blue felt headdress, holding a baby doll in my arms. I was playing one of the greatest roles of all time, at least according to my mom. I was in love with the stage and all the attention it granted me.

In the winter, the trees were covered with snow—beautiful, cold, and mysterious in every way. Some people describe North Dakota winters as great tundra. No matter how cold it was, I went outside and ran through the snow, pretending to be an Indian princess looking for shelter, ice skating on a frozen pond, sledding down the small white banks of snow, or jumping on the back of my brother's snowmobile to go for a ride. The winters were long and cold, but there was something special about experiencing them.

My chapped face reminded me that despite its sparkling beauty, snow could bring about danger, even death.

After a long day of playing outside, wrapped from head to toe in winter gear, I loved to walk through the door and smell the aroma of sugar cookies baking in the oven. I would run upstairs, with my ice-cold hands and rosy-red cheeks, and sit down at the table, and my mom would give me a big, warm cookie sprinkled with sugar. There was a sense of security in the taste and smell of those sugar cookies. They said love.

Cooperstown had a little, old grade school that always seemed to smell like mold. Living in a town with lots of snow in the winter meant using the mud rooms most of the year. We would come in from morning recess with our snow gear on, wrapped from head to toe. I stood there, trying to thaw out, watching Travis and Dean, the two cutest boys in my grade, drying off. I hurriedly took off my snow gear so I could try to look cute in my regular clothes. In the winter, fashion was whatever color your snowsuit was and whether your boots had a little wedge heel on them.

As a little girl I had a few insecurities that seemed huge at the time. I was a little on the thick side, which meant I had a round, plump face. I also had curly reddish-blonde hair and a lisp. Yep, a lisp. So I couldn't pronounce words with S's in them, which made me sound strange. I saw these things as ugly flaws and wished I could just be perfect and beautiful.

My first crush was on Travis. He was small compared to some of the other boys, with sandy-blond hair, lots of freckles, and missing teeth. He was in my second-grade class, and I sat in class and stared at him with puppy-dog eyes. I waited for him to look at me or come over and talk, even if it was just to ask for a pencil. Being "in love" with Travis made every day at school exciting.

When Valentine's Day came, I knew this was my chance. Since Travis and I were in class together, we got to share valentines with each other. I worked on my valentines box for weeks, decorating it in smooth, shiny tin foil with pink and red hearts. Now, which valentine would be his? Would he have a special one for me? What would I wear for the big Valentine's Day party? This, of course, would be decided by my mom, who brought in a new outfit she recently made. There it was, my nightmare—a long red-and-white candy-striper top and a pair of navy-blue polyester pants. What was she thinking? It wasn't the Fourth of July!

"Please," I begged her, "don't make me wear this. Please!" But she did. And it got worse when she came in to do my hair. She wrapped my pigtails into Princess Leia buns so tight I could barely feel my head! Standing in front of the mirror, looking at myself, I shook my head in frustration as tears welled up in my eyes. I saw a chubby little girl wearing an ugly outfit with donut-looking buns on both sides of her head.

I arrived at school with my valentines box in hand and wiped away my tears. As I entered the snow room, there was Travis. I started to unravel my snow gear very slowly, and when I finally got it all off, Travis walked by and said, "You look nice today."

Did I really hear that? Did Travis just compliment me? Hearing those sweet words come out of Travis's mouth made my mother my hero. And I couldn't wait to see what my valentine from Travis would look like.

Our Valentine's Day class party began, and it was time for everyone to hand out their valentines with special treats attached. As I handed mine out, I kept my eyes on Travis, anxiously watching him make his way around the room until he came to me. My heart pounded in my chest as he stopped in front of my valentines box and dropped in a card. But my heart sank as I realized it was the same card he had handed to everyone else. And there wasn't even a treat attached.

Sitting there in shock, I watched as he made his way over to my friend Gina, handing her his last and most special valentine, with a large candy heart attached. Watching the two lovebirds stare at each other was difficult to bear, so I began sorting through my box of cards. I was completely heartbroken. In my eyes Travis had chosen Gina because she was perfect—tall, thin, with long, flowy, beautiful brown hair.

Sitting next to my mom, crying over my first love and first heartbreak, she told me it would pass. And it did—when I noticed I was taller than Travis, and that his friend Dean was actually cuter.

Winter was full of frozen fun, but I was always excited for summer. It was time to put away the snowsuits and pull out the mosquito spray and shorts. Even though we lived in a small town, there was always something going on, like a town fair or street parade. The days were long and I could play outside from the time I crawled out of bed until almost ten o'clock at night.

At the end of my street was a large cul-de-sac that bled into the tree line. There was a house that sat back there where several of my friends lived. We were always creating outdoor games like "Kick the Bucket," which was basically hide-and-seek but we added a bucket. Whoever got to the bucket first, kicked it, and screamed, "Kick the bucket," was the winner. These silly games made for hours of fun as we ran and laughed outside.

Toward the end of summer, my mom took my brother and me to Red Willow, a cool little campground with a roller-skating rink. I pulled into the camp, curious to see what friends would be there from home and if any of the new friends from the summer before would be coming again. I rolled down the window of the car and breathed in the delicious aroma of hot dogs, hamburgers, greasy fries, and vanilla ice cream.

It was the summer *Grease* came out, and all I could think about were the Pink Ladies with their amazing satin jackets, Olivia Newton John's shiny black outfit, singing with leather-jacket-clad bad boy John Travolta, and the music that forever changed a generation. There was also Scott Baio, Leif Garret, Shaun Cassidy, Andy Gibb, and many more heartthrobs in silk pants and jackets. I put on my roller skates, went to the rink with flashing lights, and lost myself skating round and round for hours to "Do Run Run," "You're the One that I Want," and other '70s hits. Life was so simple. And at such a young age with a larger-than-life imagination, music, films, and heartthrobs played a huge role in my life.

One beautiful morning my mother took me out on the back patio and helped me set up my Barbie city. As always, she told me to play while she cleaned and to not leave the patio or I would be in big trouble. After she walked into the house and closed the sliding door behind her, I tried my best to play. But within a few minutes I was bored, so I ran down the stairs and jumped on my bike.

With the sun on my face and the North Dakota breeze drifting across my body and blowing through my hair, I rode to the courthouse as fast as I could to see what my dad was doing. He was busy, as usual, so I jumped back on my bike and rode to the house across the street, where one of my favorite buddies lived. I jumped off my bike, letting it drop to the ground, and ran up the dirty, paint-chipped stairs, then knocked on the broken screen door. Within seconds the boy with bright red hair and freckles, who looked like he belonged in the Little Rascals gang, welcomed me in.

As I walked through the door, everything seemed normal, but dark and a little unkempt. He introduced me to his teenage cousin who was visiting from out of town. Within a few minutes the older cousin had an idea of what we should do. "Why don't we play a game called doctor?"

I walked into my friend's bedroom, ready to play this new game. The cousin told me to lie down on the bed. When I did, he pretended to listen to my heart. Then he checked my pulse and used a popsicle stick to look in my mouth. Suddenly he started touching me where he shouldn't have. I became scared and anxious, unable to move. All of a sudden I felt pain and realized he had placed something inside me. It was the popsicle stick.

I started crying, jumped up, and ran outside to my bike. With tears streaming down my face, I could barely see as I took off riding as fast as I could, my bottom hurting badly. I kept thinking, *What am I going to tell my mom?*

Next thing I knew, she pulled up beside me. She stopped the car, jumped out, and yelled at me, until I told her the little white lie. "I fell on the bar of my bike and I'm hurting so bad." Her face softened as she went from anger to concern. The lecture quickly stopped as she began taking care of me.

I realized that with one small lie I could "fix" things—getting out of trouble but also keeping my mother from knowing the awful truth.

2

Hot Child in the City

>|◄◇►|◄

"To me, being grown-up meant smoking cigarettes, drinking cocktails and dressing up in
high heels and glamorous outfits."

LORNA LUFT

*I loved the taste of cigarettes. Taking out the pack I stole from
my dad, I gently pulled out one of the long, white, slim sticks, put
it in my mouth, grabbed my matches, and lit it until it glowed.
Taking a deep breath, I inhaled the smoke, which was like the
sweet taste of adulthood…or so I thought.*

was ten years old when my parents decided to move. We left the
plains of Cooperstown, North Dakota, on an icy-cold morning
and moved to sunny, warm Phoenix, Arizona. I was sad to leave
my friends but excited to move to a new place.

Driving across the state lines, beautiful mountains and palm
trees made up the beautiful landscape of our new home. We had
visited Phoenix several times since my grandparents moved there
a few years earlier. We moved in with them for a short time while
my parents looked for a home. Jimmie Carter was president, and

it was a tough time to buy a house because of the high interest rates.

My brother, Randy, and I attended the elementary school down the street. We both jumped right in. I was still a little on the thick side, which meant I had bigger boobs in third grade than I did going into junior high. For some reason this made me a target, and despite trying to fit in, I always felt like I didn't belong.

Randy found his way much faster than I did. He was good-looking, cool, and a really nice guy. The boys wanted to be friends with him and the girls wanted to date him. The nice part about having a popular older brother was that the older boys would look out for me and the older girls were nice to me so they could get closer to Randy.

Eventually my parents found a home a few miles away from my grandparents. Although it wasn't the area where my mom wanted to live in, it was what we could afford, which meant the home needed a lot of TLC. My parents let me finish school by my grandparents' house so I didn't have to make a change in the middle of the year.

I started sixth grade just around the corner from our new house. The excitement of starting anew quickly dissipated as I realized most of the sixth graders had gone to school together since kindergarten and there was no room in their cliques for another girl. Needless to say, I wasn't very happy at my new school and ended up being the target.

My mother always dressed me nicely. She would save all her money and take me shopping for clothes. But walking into the classroom with my new cool multicolored sweater and pastel pink cords didn't make a good first impression with the other girls. I really tried to be part of my new school, but it just wasn't going to happen. So instead I focused on trying to make friends outside of school, around my neighborhood.

Hot Child in the City

I became friends with one girl, Sara, who had a lot of the same likes as I did—music and pretending to be older than we were. She had a couple of brothers and a sister. I loved going over to her house to hang out. Her brothers were artists and loved music, so we would sit in their room, smoking cigarettes we stole from our parents, and listening to Pat Benatar's "Love Is a Battle-field," "Hell Is for Children," and "Hit Me with Your Best Shot." I spent hours at her house, or as long as my mother would let me stay, dreaming of being a rock star.

I had grown up watching old Hollywood musicals—*Seven Brides for Seven Brothers, Oklahoma,* and *Hair.* Music and movies ruled my world, allowing me to live in a fantasy. I could be whomever I wanted.

On one of the last afternoons I remember spending with Sara, we watched a movie called *The Apple,* a cheesy film about a rock star in the future. I sat with my eyes glued to the TV, watching every minute, dreaming of being that girl in the movie. She wanted everything and was willing to sell her soul to take a bite of that apple. I wanted her life. I wanted the guy to sing to me and have everyone cheer for our love. I was completely seduced by the illusion of happiness and success of Hollywood movies. I knew then and there I had to find my rock star.

I spent a lot of time with my older cousin, Jodi, who lived in Phoenix. Growing up, Jodi and I spent time together in North Dakota at family gatherings. She and I loved performing for the aunts and uncles—Captain and Tennille, Donnie and Marie—we always had a show to do. Jodi was a beautiful blonde, and she had the most amazing eyelashes. I loved sitting and watching her feather her hair and use her Maybelline mascara. I wanted to be just like Jodi and copied everything she did. She wore super-cool flared jeans with a rainbow on the pocket and OP T-shirts. She was the essence of cool, and by default that made me cool.

31

Jodi often invited me to the neighborhood park to hang with her friends. No one was old enough to drive, so we walked. Sometimes it was already dark when we headed up to the park, but my mom would let me go because I was with Jodi. We would meet up with the Bigelow boys, and others from the neighborhood, lighting up stolen cigarettes and feeling like the luckiest girls in the neighborhood. The Bigelow boys were terribly cute but terrible trouble for a young girl like me. It was like jumping headfirst into a pool of temptation. And I loved every minute of it.

I was crazy about Brian Bigelow from the minute I first laid eyes on him. Tall, dark, and handsome, I thought he liked me the way I liked him and that we were in love, like Sandy and Danny in *Grease*, Claude and Sheila in *Hair*, or Alphie and Bibi in *The Apple*. Ah, the puppy love of a young girl, the feeling of meaning something to someone. We spent hours together just walking. Brian didn't live far from my cousin Jodi, so it was easy to get to him. We would put on our roller skates and head over to the Bigelow house to hang out. Their parents were rarely home, which meant no adult supervision. That made it too easy to be bad.

The naïveté of childhood produces innocence, but that same naïveté can gets kids into trouble. One day of "hanging out" changed my world. This time the normal flirting escalated, and before I knew it, I was in Brian's bedroom, raging with hormones and having feelings I had never felt before. I was in love and thought I would be with Brian for the rest of my life.

My desire to be an adult, while still being a child, led me to make childlike decisions about adult things. Lying on his bed I kept thinking how much he loved me. I was scared but thought, *I'm ready.* We still had our clothes on but he managed to pull the covers over us, covering not only our bodies but the reality of what was going on. He continued to kiss me, and before I knew it we were having sex. I had crossed the line and could never go back.

I was willing to give up something beautiful and sacred for the sake of love, or the flawed idea that I told myself was love. But being young, I didn't value my purity. I didn't realize how precious it was and that once it was lost, I would never be able to get it back. I was so wrapped up in the illusion of a Hollywood romance, I was willing to offer up my innocence to become an "adult," like the leading ladies I had seen on the movie screen.

It all happened so fast. And our relationship was over even faster. The romance ended as soon as the pants came down.

I found myself once again sitting in my bedroom, trying to forget everything, drowning in the music of the '80s. Listening to Air Supply's "The One that You Love" a hundred times over, I cried my heart out over my first love, thinking my life was over.

But as quickly as the next love song hit the airway, I was on my way to the park again as if nothing happened.

Summer between sixth grade and seventh was the beginning of many changes, the first being my physical appearance. My face and body started taking on a whole new look. My chubby body turned into a more athletic one as my round baby face began looking more mature. I was thrilled and welcomed the change as I started my new middle school.

Middle school started off better than sixth grade, and I decided to try out for the pom line, performing my routine to "Kung-Fu Fighting." I loved the thought of being able to dance at school, but I didn't make the cut and I was devastated. But twenty-four hours later, my parents received a call inviting me to be part of the pom line. I really didn't care why or what happened. The only thing that mattered was that I was on the squad.

Things took a turn when the most popular boy at school started to like me. But what seemed like a good thing quickly turned awful. Rumors started to spread like the flu and felt just as bad. The girls told stories that I'd let him do things with me and we had sex, but it wasn't true. The rumors broke me. I cried every morning before school. When my mother caught on, she became furious about the bullying. She was my biggest cheerleader and immediately went to bat for me. She confronted the school, but nobody did anything to help bring this terrible situation to an end. So she put me back into my old school by my grandparents' house. I was finally happy.

During this intense time, my mom decided to get my brother and me back into church. We went to a Bible church that preached a strong message about heaven or hell. "Where do you want to go?" the pastor often asked. When he offered a way to get into heaven, I raised my hand because I sure didn't want to go to hell. But I later found out this meant becoming a member of the church and getting baptized.

As the old became the new, my new kept holding on to the old, and my rebirth was over before it started. I tried to get involved with the church youth group, but I didn't feel like I belonged. I had already lived such a different life. I wasn't the young girl wearing bobby socks. I had already graduated into heels. So instead I headed for the ice-skating rink at Metro Center, where the older crowd hung out. My type, the kind who loved rock music, smoking, and having a good time. The misfits and the rebels. They looked perfect to me.

A few weeks after returning to my old school, I found myself back in the not-so-good graces of the popular girls, challenged by the leader, who decided she didn't like me and wanted everyone else to hate me as well. Closing my locker one day, I came face-to-face with Shawn and her clique. Estrogen was flying everywhere. Before I knew what had happened, she slapped me across the face. Not thinking, I grabbed the door to my locker and slammed her head into it. Before either one of us could go any further, we were sitting in the principal's office, explaining what happened.

What we didn't expect was that we would enter the office as enemies but leave as best friends. We walked out of there talking about doing something together after school. Even our mothers became friends. My mom was looking for a part-time job and Shawn's mom was looking for an assistant for a medical management office. It worked out perfectly...until some unethical stuff went down. Then my mom decided to go back to staying at home.

Shawn and I were into the same things. We loved cool clothes, hair, makeup, and anything rock 'n' roll. Shawn was a natural beauty and looked very mature for her age. She had the coolest feathered hair, olive skin, perfect white teeth, and a fashion sense that killed! She was beautiful yet edgy, a total rocker chick. Meanwhile, I was packing on makeup, never sure of who I was—the rocker chick, or the sweet little girl who still had rainbow sheets and unicorns on her wall.

I pulled Shawn into my world of skating, and we spent a lot of time at the mall, on the rink, eating ice cream at Farrell's, and perusing incredibly cool clothing stores like Merry-Go-Round. My life seemed to be just like the name of my favorite store, and as I walked through it, longing for the next pair of parachute pants, I dreamed of working there and selling cool clothes to the rockers who shopped there.

After shopping we usually headed down to the ice-skating rink. Walking down the staircase and into the lobby of the rink, the cold air hit me like a shot of adrenaline. I wore hockey skates at the rink, which gave me an in right away with the cool older crowd, many of them boys. With their long hair, colorful parachute pants, and leather jackets, I was hooked watching them skate to songs like the Scorpions' "Rock You like a Hurricane" and "Rhythm of Love."

Skating the rink with the lights dim and the rock music blaring, I found comfort and solitude. It was a place I could lose myself to Journey, Heart, Bay City Rollers, and Warrant. Every time I listened to the radio, some incredible song would come on I could totally relate to. I listened to Alta Nova's "Fantasy" over and over again, dreaming of being a famous model married to a rock star or hockey player. My goal was to find Mr. Right and live the cover-girl life. I was in love with the glamorous world of big hair and rock 'n' roll.

The ice-skating rink had the perfect world of ice and guys who loved rock 'n' roll like I did. Watching the girls and guys skate to the music under the dim lights, highlighting the blue of the ice, I waited for my handsome ice-skating rocker to ask me to join him on the rink to a slow song. I always left the rink after a long, fun night, dreaming of the next weekend when I could skate again.

One night, Shawn and I headed to the mall to listen to a live band play music while we ice skated. My mom drove us. When we picked up Shawn, she looked like a rocker chick in her red parachute pants, an extremely cool black-and-white T-shirt, heels, and hair feathered back. I always seemed to feel "less than," especially around Shawn, and went through a moment of comparing.

We arrived at the skating rink, and it was packed with well-dressed, big-haired teenagers. The band was rocking as we pushed our way to the front row, excited to see the hot band members. With our eyes on the lead singer and lead guitar player, we flirted like crazy, thinking we would get them for sure. But as the night wound down, we realized it wasn't going to happen.

As Shawn and I made our way to the back of the rink, we came across two good-looking older guys. Shawn pointed out that one of them looked like Steve Perry and immediately went over to flirt with him, leaving me with the friend. His name was Don. The first thing I noticed about him was his great hair, dark and feathered back perfectly. He had brown eyes, a nice smile, dimples, and a great sense of style. He looked extremely sharp in a dark leather jacket, Jordache jeans, and white loafers with little tassels.

While Shawn worked her magic on Steve, Don and I got to know each other. He had just graduated from high school and got a job teaching people how to use computers. I was impressed by his ambition, his good looks, and his charm.

Next thing I knew we were walking to the car and Don was giving us a ride home. The last seat was up front next to Don, and as I slid across, I felt happy, like I had been chosen. He flashed me a big, beautiful smile and put the car into drive. We were off on a ride that would change my life.

On the way home, I didn't feel unsure, just charmed by Don's wit and self-assurance. He shared with me about his family and where he had gone to high school. He was a ways from his side of town, but that didn't seem to matter. He told me about his parents and where they came from, his likes and dislikes about people and places. I hinged on every word he shared and smiled like I totally knew what he was talking about, throwing in an occasional giggle.

The ride home seemed to go fast. One minute we were pulling out of the parking lot of Metro Center, and the next we were sitting in front of my house. My dad's cop car wasn't there, so I knew I had a few minutes to get inside without a worry.

Getting out of that car with Don, I felt years older. I walked around to the other side, opened my purse, and pulled out a pen and paper. I handed him my number as we said our good-byes— no kiss, just a long, deep look into his big brown eyes. Then I took out the pack of cigarettes I'd stolen from my dad, gently pulled one out, and lit it until it glowed. I took a deep breath and inhaled the smoke, basking in the hazy fog that masked whatever innocence I had left. I watched my childhood waft away with each exhale, glad to see it go. Little did I know, this night would change my life, making me grow up and face adulthood much too quickly. The cigarette burned hot…and so, I thought, would my future.

3

Two-Faced Love

>–⊷–◦–◦⊷–◦

"Love makes you do crazy things, insane things.
Things in a million years you never thought
you'd see yourself do."

BRANDON BOYCE, *WICKER PARK*

There I stood in the elevator, watching the doors close in front of me. I had just received the biggest news of my life. As I gazed at the reflection staring back at me on those steel doors, I thought, This is not how I imagined my life as a teenager. Full of fear, joy, sadness, and disbelief, I ruminated over everything—high school, marriage, my future. What was I going to do now?

Life with Don was a roller coaster and I was enjoying the ride. I started high school with him as my boyfriend. Despite a few ups and downs, we seemed to coast most of the time, especially in the beginning. We had been together for a year and he had a job teaching people how to use computers. I thought he was brilliant, and all of my girlfriends envied me because I had an older boyfriend with a car and a job.

Although my dreams of being a supermodel weren't coming true, and I was consumed with love for a man who was nothing close to being a rock star, teenage life seemed exciting. Don and I were together in every way, which meant we were having sex. It was a real relationship and I didn't feel like I was in high school. We spent many evenings at my house, lying on the couch like we were married, then I'd walk into my bedroom and be hit by the reality of a fourteen-year-old girl. Surrounded by my white-tufted, twin-sized waterbed with rainbow bedding, I could never go back to the innocence of childhood. I had left it all far behind me.

Youth and naïveté made it difficult to recognize the juxtaposition of my double life, one as a teenager surrounded by a bedroom of unicorns, the other consisting of dates with Don, sneaking into bars and going places I shouldn't. On nights that Don would get restless and want to go out, I'd walk into my bedroom and turn on my boom box, hoping to find a song that would speak to me. I sat down in front of a little white vanity, put on blue eye shadow, and gave my cheeks just the right amount of blush—which at my age meant way too much. From there I moved on to the hair. It had to be curled and feathered just right. I transformed from fourteen to eighteen in a matter of minutes, ready to be by Don's side.

When Don walked into a room, I watched in amazement at his electricity. He had this charisma that made everyone turn and look. Everyone wanted to be next to him. But soon I discovered that this charming man could turn into a crazy monster in a matter of seconds if something hit him wrong. I never knew what would set him off and when fists would fly. I only had to watch it happen once to know what Don's face looked like when he was ready to take on the room and everyone in it. It was somewhat terrifying at times, but also exhilarating knowing I had this "bad boy" as my boyfriend.

I managed to keep all of my late-night escapades a secret from my mom and dad. This seemed like a good idea, so they wouldn't worry or lose their image of the daughter they'd brought up "right." Just as Don could work a room, he could also work my parents, and they would let me go anywhere as long as I was with him. He charmed his way into their good graces with wild, often sad stories about his family, laughing them off like they weren't a big deal while my parents' hearts were breaking for him, wondering how they could help this troubled young man.

When things went well I looked forward to spending as much time as possible with Don. But when things got bad, they were really bad. I especially noticed changes in Don when he was with his brothers. Don felt the same way about being with them as I did when I was with him—invincible, unbreakable, and full of high-octane adrenaline. He worshipped them and everything they represented. Unfortunately, they were nothing but trouble. Despite looking different from Don on the outside, with their T-shirts and steel-toed boots and riding their motorcycles, on the inside they were very much the same.

One of Don's brothers had recently returned from prison, and Don looked up to him like a hero. As Don started to hang out with his brother I noticed something different about his behavior, which affected our relationship. Out of nowhere he started huge fights with me over the phone, one minute saying he never wanted to see me again, the next calling to apologize and profess his love. Later he showed up at my house and stayed for a couple of days, sitting in the kitchen, smiling and eating waffles, acting like the young man he should have had time to be. He laughed and joked, without a care in the world. It was like nothing had happened.

I began to believe our problems were because of things that I did or didn't do. I never knew who or what I was going to get, which at that age was very intimidating and confusing.

One cold night, after it had rained all day, Don took me to a bar hangout. There was a band playing, and he knew several of his friends would be there. Too naïve to recognize the emotionally dangerous web I was tangled in, I held on to the hope that Don would treat me the way he did when we first started dating.

After a short time, I headed to the ladies' room. When I came out, the band had taken a break and Don stood at the bar, talking with some guy I didn't recognize. I recognized the look on Don's face. Sure enough, moments later, his fist pounded into the guy. The bouncers came running and tried to grab Don, but he fought back. Before I knew what had happened, he grabbed me and we went flying through the front door into the cold, pouring rain, running for our lives toward the car. He kept telling me to run faster, but my spiked heels could only go so fast. He pushed me in and we took off. My black winged eyeliner was running down my face, I was soaking wet, cold and shaking, scared to death, not sure what was happening.

Later I sat in the corner of my bedroom crying, wondering how I got to where I was. The duplicity of my life was starting to get to me. I was pretending to be one way by day and another by night, lying to my parents and losing myself in the meantime. I was fourteen, smoking like a chimney, having sex, and being manipulated into thinking I was a terrible person if I mistrusted Don or wanted too much from him.

I was too young to realize Don was mentally abusive. I loved him, and I'd given him everything, every part of me. I convinced myself things would get better, and I was eager to please him. But the one person who was supposed to make me feel safe had become the biggest danger of all.

As my freshman year came to an end, so did my relationship with Don. He and his brother had gotten into some serious trouble again. This time a terrible fight had happened and there were several people who had been hurt pretty badly, so Don and his brother had to leave the state. Don's brother was on parole and didn't want to go back to jail. They both headed for New Orleans, running from the law to escape the possibility of going to jail.

I was a wreck. There were so many emotions that I was trying to get ahold of. My heart broke knowing my "bad boy" was gone and he might soon forget me. But I wanted to be there for him. I wanted him to be happy, so I tried to stay positive and did my best to handle all of this like an adult. A long-distance relationship began, and we spoke daily, professing our love for each other.

As time went on, it became harder and harder to catch Don at home. I was putting my life on hold, sitting around waiting for him to call. The physical distance created emotional distance and we began speaking less. I figured he had lost interest in me, and to be honest, I was losing interest in him. The more time that passed, the easier it was to see life more clearly.

Don and his brother seemed to be right at home with their family in New Orleans, going out and having a good time. The fear of dating other guys began wearing off as Don and his brother were living in a new state, and I began to see my life in a whole new way.

Things were different as I started my sophomore year at Greenway. I had a couple of really close girlfriends whom I hung out with. I had known Kim since junior high and she always made me laugh, cracking jokes while driving her Pinto. Julie, a blonde bombshell, and I met in the cafeteria my freshman year and have been friends ever since. And there was Renee, the green-eyed beauty whom I got to know and bonded which quickly after finding out our families both came from North Dakota.

I also made the cheer team and enjoyed wearing the green-and-gold uniform, excited to be part of my school. One of the varsity football players liked me, and I was becoming part of the popular crowd. It felt like I belonged, and I finally had a chance to be a normal teenager.

Still, hanging out with high school friends didn't seem like enough. I had been living this other life, this grown-up life, and before long, I started getting tired of all the high school drama, going to high school parties and fighting over the popular football jock. One minute some high school boy liked you, and the next, he was chasing after his next conquest passing by him in the halls.

The time apart from Don opened up the possibility of having a new relationship, and as a young girl raging with hormones, I badly wanted the security of a boyfriend. I was used to having a serious boyfriend, and it seemed easier to second-guess a relationship than never know if you were really in one or not. So I was already on the lookout for something new. And before I knew it, I found it.

My brother and several of the best-looking grads from Greenway worked at the local gas station. Every girl I knew from Greenway made it a point to get gas a couple of times a week or just stop in to get the windows cleaned. One of my brother's best friends, Robert, made getting gas a real joy, even if I was in the car with my mom. Robert was tall, dark, and incredibly handsome. He was one of those guys who actually looked better dirty, in his uniform with a little grease on his face and sweat on his brow. Pulling up to the full-service gas station, rolling down the window, and leaning on the door, I couldn't wait for him to pump my gas.

Robert started to hang out more and more at my house. My brother had put some weights in our garage, and they spent hours working out while I spent hours trying to figure out how to talk to Robert. I loved sneaking out to the garage while they were working out just to get a quick glimpse of his buffed body.

He noticed me as well, and after flirting like crazy for a while, we started hanging out. We went to parties together, and before I knew it, I was telling little white lies to my mom so I could spend the night with Robert. We had a heated romance and I started to come alive again. There was something about waking up next to this gorgeous man who looked at me with deep compassion that made me feel beautiful. It was something I had never experienced with Don, and I began falling hard.

I was just starting to get used to my new normal life with Robert when one day Don showed up, unannounced and very possessive. His brother had been dating someone in Phoenix before they had to jump states and head to New Orleans, and he had been hoping to get back to Arizona to continue his romance. Before long, both Don and his brother were on their way back, and Don expected nothing to have changed between us. It was a strange new twist on our nonexistent relationship. He tried to woo me. And when that didn't work, he stalked me, often parking under the streetlight outside my house, waiting for me to return from a party. I didn't want to be with Don anymore. I had Robert and I was happy. But Don wasn't used to taking no for an answer, especially from me.

I had love in my eyes after spending the night with Robert. Needing a ride home, he grabbed his roommate's keys and took me for a spin in a T-top Corvette. I felt so free, like a real teenager, enjoying my life to the fullest. My life was exactly the way I wanted it. We took the roof off, cranked up the music, and flew down the road, talking about the upcoming party Randy and I were going to throw with some of our Greenway friends. Our parents were away for the night, and we intended to take full advantage of that. I didn't know it at the time, but it would be my last morning with Robert.

That evening Randy and I had everything ready for our small

get-together. I had a new white-and-black dress with a red pat-ent-leather belt, which I hoped would make a statement and keep Robert staring at me all night. The party quickly grew, and our small get-together became a huge, out-of-control party. People poured in from both the front door and the back gate, wandering through our house, making themselves at home. The loud music combined with the escalating chatter of the crowd was deafening. All I could think about was spending some quiet time with Rob-ert. But when I went to look for him, he was nowhere to be found.

I walked around the house, in the backyard, then around to the front, making my way through the sea of people, but I didn't see Robert anywhere. I went back into the house, and within min-utes I saw him emerge from the back bedrooms with an unsettled look. I was confused until I saw Don following a few feet behind. I tried to talk to Robert, but he quickly left the party. Then, with-out missing a beat, Don took his place in my house with me, thrusting me back into the past I thought I had left behind.

It wasn't until the following day that I found out what hap-pened that night. Robert shared with me that Don lured him into my bedroom, then held a knife to his throat. He warned him to stay away from me or he would kill Robert. Robert feared Don would actually do it. He had seen Don fight and didn't want to cross him. My beautiful romance with Robert was over, and I started to believe I had no life outside of Don.

Life continued as if Don had never left and the past six months had never happened. My complacency made it extremely difficult to make a change, and being so young I didn't have the confidence to stand up for myself or the experience to even know to do it. So instead I found myself content with the comfort of what I knew and how I had lived for so long. Once again, I began losing myself in order to make someone else happy.

I started to spend all of my time with Don. Wherever he went,

I went. I was used to this from before, and it seemed natural for it to happen again. I found myself thinking of a life with him that could turn out right this time.

Summer came and we started spending more time with Don's family. I was beginning to enjoy my time with them. Don's sister, who was a hairdresser, offered to do my hair for me. I sat for several hours talking about life and laughing at stories she shared about their childhood. She had just finished the highlights when it was time to head out and go home. Don and I got in the car and headed toward my parents' house when he told me that he had to make a stop. We ended up at an apartment building near my parents' house, right behind a church our family had attended a few times. I was familiar with the area and didn't think twice about it.

We parked, then started our climb up the flight of stairs to an apartment. Don knocked, and when the door opened, the smell of alcohol permeated the air as a bedraggled man in his late twenties, early thirties, spoke to us, telling us to come in. I immediately felt uneasy, clinging to Don's side as we walked in.

Inside, there was an insidious-looking woman standing in the kitchen, cutting up food, keeping her eyes on us as I sat on a barstool at the counter and Don stood by the table, making small talk with the guy. Suddenly, the woman started yelling at the guy to stop staring at me. I looked at her in disbelief and tried to reassure her that he wasn't staring at me. Scared, I kept shaking my head. A terrible fear took over my entire being, and a cold chill ran from the top of my head to the tips of my toes.

The woman grabbed a butcher knife and came flying around the corner toward me. In a split second I was out of my seat, rushing for the door. I threw it open and sped down the stairs, terrified she would catch up to me. I had nowhere to go, and no keys to get into the car, so I ran as fast as I could through the apartment complex parking lot, adrenaline pumping through my body. She chased after me, screaming, with the knife in her hand. I turned quickly to see how close she was, and was relieved to see Don charging after her. Don grabbed her, wrestled her to the ground, and took the knife away. After yelling at me to stop, Don turned his attention to the crazy woman, shouting at her while keeping her constrained. The guy came up behind them, seizing the woman and telling us to leave. I was trembling with fear, tears streaming down my face. I felt like my life had just passed before my eyes. But Don had saved me, and in some odd way this made him a hero to me.

Eventually, Don and I became engaged. I don't remember the proposal. I think I was in a daze and had no idea what was happening. But at the time, that seemed normal. There was a side of me that wanted to be married and not have to worry about the drama of dating, what my girlfriends thought, or my parents telling me what to do. I was a rebel, a free spirit, different from others. But this wasn't what I pictured my life looking like. Don was no rock star or hockey player. But he was a bad boy I found attractive, even if he was destructive to me.

I tried to forget about any of the negative things that happened between Don and me, and focused instead on planning our wedding. Despite our age difference, everyone seemed excited for Don and me, and Don's family often came alongside to help. Being a silly teenage girl, all I could think about was having red and white wedding colors, wearing a hat, and carrying a bouquet of red roses. I wanted my dress to be big and stunning, like Cinderella's. My biggest concern was the fashion statement my dress would make and I wanted to look beautiful. I was thrilled to be getting married, thinking I would no longer have to deal with high school pettiness. I reserved the church, picked out decorations, put together wedding announcements, and shared with my friends the exciting news that I was getting married.

Since I was a junior in high school, some people thought I was crazy, while others assumed I was pregnant and had to get married. But many of my girlfriends who had difficult home lives seemed envious of what I was doing and wanted the same freedom I had.

Although marriage meant being free from parental rules and guidelines, my freedom was not my own. We did whatever Don wanted to do, whenever he wanted to do it. When it was time to go out, it was always with Don's friends, never mine. I was always preparing myself to look like an adult, to fit in with the people we were hanging out with. I became whatever Don wanted me to be. I sat down in front of my little vanity mirror, looking like a teenager. And within a few minutes, with a brush of blush, a smudge of eye shadow, and a bold lipstick, I was transformed and ready to go.

One Friday night, Don told me we were going to a party. I got ready, as usual. After driving downtown to the seedy part of Phoenix, we pulled up to a rundown duplex. It was dark and dirty. Don turned off the car and told me we had arrived at the party. I got out of the car, looking around for something or someone to make it seem like a safe place, or at least like a party was going on. But there was nothing. I felt completely uncomfortable, and a sinking feeling grew deep in my stomach. I didn't want to go in. But Don grabbed me and shoved me through the door.

The place was a rat-hole, a drug house where two men and a woman, all addicts, were waiting for Don. They were the party. The small duplex walls were yellow from smoke, the ragged carpet was thin and torn. The woman lit up a cigarette, creating a thick haze in the room. I looked through the smoke to see a filthy bed, a sagging recliner, and a kitchen cluttered with trash. Don told me to sit down on the bed. Though disgusted by the rancid aroma of filth, I did as I was told, not wanting to cause problems.

My mind flashed back to the woman with the butcher knife,

and I feared that one of these people could hurt me as well. I became nonexistent as Don began snorting cocaine and drinking alcohol. Scared, exhausted, and feeling like a piece of trash, all I could do was sit there and think, *What have I chosen for my life?* There was nothing beautiful or glamorous about any of this. I was broken and flawed, a young woman who had given her life to a controlling, manipulative drug addict.

After a few hours, I got up and asked Don to take me home. He glared at me, telling me to sit back down on the bed because he wasn't ready to leave. I tried to keep a tough front, lighting a cigarette, silently stewing to myself. Eventually I fell asleep. When I woke early the next morning, Don was still snorting cocaine, but I could tell the supply was finally coming to an end. His eyes were glassy like marbles, his complexion a chalky gray.

Though I was fearful of what my parents might say when we returned home, Don quickly eased my mother's worries. When we walked through the door, he pulled himself together, threw on a smile, and lied about what we had been doing. She bought the line he told her, wanting to believe that Don had my best interest at heart and would never let anything or anyone hurt me.

I refrained from telling my parents anything bad that happened with Don. We were engaged, and my mom was looking at me more like a married woman than a little girl. So it was easy for her to accept Don and his stories.

The prospect of marriage brought along a spirit of hope, happiness, and love. I truly believed that once I married Don, things would get better and I would be happy. I saw marriage as a fresh start, the end of my duplicitous life, as Don and I would come together as one. I believed he would stop any bad behavior and that we would live happily ever after as husband and wife. I figured that if he was happy, I would be happy too.

My wedding day finally came and it was beautiful. Everything was done in red and white, just like I had envisioned. I was crazy with nerves as I prepared to walk down the aisle. Putting on my hat and connecting it to my perfectly feathered hair, it suddenly hit me that I was getting married and I was still in high school. Taking one last look in the long wardrobe mirror, I started thinking about Don, hoping he would find me breathtaking.

I made my grand entrance into the church, looking over at Don standing there, clean cut in his white suit, accessorized with red accents and a perfect smile, looking gorgeous, like he did the night I met him. I walked in with my Cinderella gown, a big hat tilted to the side, and red roses. I looked around the room and saw the faces of high school friends, my family, Don's family, and his friends. My dad stood by my side as I prepared to take the first step toward the altar. I didn't walk down the aisle feeling like a frivolous teenager, but like a mature young woman ready to step into a new world.

We returned to my parents' house for the reception, a fun night of dancing, cake, and love. I had fallen for Don all over again. He always had a way of doing that to me. It felt so surreal, with everything and everyone seeming to move in slow motion, an exceptional night celebrating what would now be my new normal. I was married!

We ate and enjoyed the company of all our family and friends. As Don's sisters passed out cake, his parents talked with family and mine greeted our guests. For the first time in a long time I was really happy. All seemed right. And as the night came to an end, I was ready to be together with Don as husband and wife.

The next morning I got up and didn't feel right. I headed straight for the bathroom. My mom was the first person I saw and I told her, "I think I'm pregnant." She looked at me with a skeptical expression, as if she didn't believed it could happen so quickly. But I knew something was different.

At the doctor's office, I took a blood test. Moments later, the doctor delivered the news: I was pregnant. I felt scared, happy, sad, and in disbelief. And my mother's face expressed the same mix of emotions. We walked to the exit in silence, and as the elevator doors closed in front of us, I stood there staring at my reflection, thoughts swirling around in my head.

Finally my mom turned to me and said, "How are we going to tell your dad?"

Part Two
THE CARNIVAL
Seeking Myself

R ound and round it goes, where it stops nobody knows. The carnival is one of the most entertaining yet strangest places on earth. Some of my fondest memories are of being a young girl waiting for the carnival to arrive. For a small-town girl with big dreams, it meant another place to lose myself. Colorful lights and loud music exuding from the rides. Smiling children and adults screaming with excitement as they bounce around. The aroma of cotton candy and Indian fry bread filling the air for miles, as warm summer days turn into fun-filled nights. These memories have lingered in my mind, dancing around and calling my name to return over and over again.

Leaving the small town and moving to the big city brought sadness as I feared I would no longer be able to enjoy the carnival. But the carnival made its way to the big city, and on a much grander scale. Everything was bigger, brighter, and more dangerously captivating. I stood in front of my favorite ride, taking it all in. The music blaring as the roller coaster went round and round, up and down. Life could spin out of control yet look so appealing, the flashing lights masking the imminent danger.

Before I knew it, I was no longer a little girl watching the roller coaster rush by, but a young woman on the ride of life, standing before men with the same inquisitive nature that led me to the carnival in the first place. Their bright smiles, sweet words, and exciting kisses, disguising the dangers of what I thought was love. One day I woke up and realized the carnival had gone, leaving me a little girl with a broken heart. I had to grow up and realize the excitement of the carnival was fleeting, and that I was merely a stop along the way.

4

Donnie's Gift

⊱⋅•⋅⊰

"Drugs are a waste of time.
They destroy your memory and your self-respect
and everything that goes along with your self-
esteem. They're no good at all."

KURT COBAIN, *ROLLING STONES* MAGAZINE

A wave of emotions washed over me like nothing I'd felt before. I walked into the bathroom shaking and struggling to breathe. It felt like I was having a heart attack, and in a way I was. Freaking out, crying, not sure what was going on, I caught my reflection in the mirror. I had lost all self-respect. I knew my life needed to change.

I looked around my bedroom, decorated with a beautiful white vanity and unicorns on the wall—everything a girl my age could want. Only now I shared it with my husband. It was 1986, I was seventeen years old, married and pregnant, beginning my senior year of high school. Don and I were living with my parents. Don wasn't making enough money to get us out on our own. But none of that mattered.

Standing in the kitchen with my parents, I told my dad I

was pregnant. He just stood there staring at me, his face blank as he started to turn pale. I don't think he knew what to say or how to feel about it, but he was clearly disappointed as he left the kitchen, retreating to his room. I leaned on the counter and lit a cigarette, feeling okay with my situation, thinking this was the next step after getting married. I wasn't planning for it to happen so quickly, but it did and I accepted it.

I never felt my school friends judging me. We all had our own issues to deal with and mine just happened to be pregnancy. One of my friends had recently welcomed a new baby brother to her family, another was living from one house to the next because of family feuding. Yet another friend had dropped out of high school and was dating an older man. My life wasn't any different really. In fact, it seemed to be right in line with everyone else's.

A few weeks into the school year, I was asked to leave Greenway and transfer to a school for pregnant teens. I didn't want to leave my friends during my senior year of high school, but I knew it was probably the best thing for me as I prepared to become a young mother.

The school was a bit of a drive, but I didn't have much choice. I hopped in my car in the morning and headed to school with music blaring, mentally preparing myself for the day ahead. I didn't love school, but it wasn't a struggle for me either, and I could get good grades if I wanted to. There were no scholarships rolling in after I started there. In fact, there was no pressure at all for me to attend college and further my education.

My days consisted of normal schoolwork and learning about motherhood. We had many conversations about becoming mothers, our choices in terms of adoption, whether or not we planned on getting married, and if we wanted to continue our education after the baby was born. Our teacher was quite supportive and wonderful, always encouraging us and believing we were capable of anything.

One by one the girls had their babies and often disappeared shortly thereafter. Whether school became too much or they went back to their old schools, I didn't know. Nobody really talked about it after they left. I was thankful my due date was close to my graduation. That way I could take the year to focus on school and my growing belly.

I learned a lot about myself during this time. I discovered that I was a fighter. The more people told me I would never finish school or amount to anything, the harder I worked to prove them wrong.

With my due date approaching quickly, I was thrilled when I was given permission to graduate with my senior class at Greenway. That meant I would get to sit and walk alongside my friends as I received my diploma.

Don's support was all right during this time. I could tell he was starting to feel pressure to work hard and make money to take care of his family. He was working long hours and trying to act like the husband and father he was now supposed to be. But no matter how hard he tried, after a short period of time he would fall off the wagon and be right back to where he started, disappearing for hours, drinking, doing drugs, and dealing with bad people.

Meanwhile, I was trying to keep it together by attending school, preparing for my baby shower, getting bigger, and trying to figure out how we were going to make enough money to move out on our own once the baby arrived.

During this year, we spent a lot of time hanging out with Don's friends. His best friend, Mike, had a girlfriend, Lisa, a tall, skinny blonde with tattoos and hair all the way down her back.

Lisa was also pregnant and having a boy, so she and I became especially close.

Despite our age difference and contrasting backgrounds, Lisa and I got along well. She was rough around the edges, a topless dancer who had lived with a biker gang in Arizona since she was thirteen years old. She shared crazy scary stories with me about how the gang members had threatened to kill her if she ever left Mike, but eventually she found a way to escape and start over. My eyes wide open and sitting on the edge of my chair, I hung on every detail as she shared about strip bars and motorcycle clubs. I was amazed by Lisa. She was doing what she knew how to do and worked hard to live independently.

Lisa was especially kind to me. I think, in some odd way, she looked at me like a little sister, someone who still had an innocence about her that she needed to protect. She always included me with her dancer friends and often chose to spend time with me even when she could be with Mike and the others who were of age, doing things I couldn't.

She had lived a hard, fast life and appreciated having her space. She didn't need to be out partying, and the last place she seemed to enjoy was a bar. There were times when the guys would go to the Gram Center Station, a popular bar perfect for a quick drink. I couldn't go in because I wasn't twenty-one, so Lisa sat outside with me and smoked while we waited for them. I enjoyed our time together, listening to the captivating tales she shared with me about her extraordinary life. We never really knew what would go down by the end of the night. Sometimes the guys would walk out after a few drinks peaceful and content, but other times they would come running out at full speed, yelling at us to start the car.

Christmas came, and it was the first time that all of my gifts were either for the baby or for the household. Then New Year's

Eve rolled around. Don and I were going to spend the evening at a party Mike and Lisa were hosting at their home. Oddly enough, it happened to be just down the street from my grandparents' old house. By this time I was showing…and starting to see the disaster my life was becoming.

As everyone celebrated New Year's Eve, I sat in my black crushed-velvet jumpsuit, thinking about the fact that I was seventeen, pregnant, and hanging out with a bunch of twenty-somethings, doing drugs and drinking like crazy. As I sat in the front room watching everything move as if in slow motion, I noticed all the pretty women wandering through the party in their slinky New Year's Eve outfits and stiletto heels, looking sexy. Everyone was drinking and laughing and enjoying each other's company, as I became nonexistent to Don and all the other party guests.

Don finally made his way over to me a minute or two before midnight, smiling, with drink in hand. He grabbed me as I stood to my feet. We waited for the clock to strike midnight, and as it did, Don kissed me as everyone cheered for the new year. Then he went right back to partying. I slept the night away on the couch.

Waking up to a new year, I was reminded of my reality—finishing high school and having a baby.

I began to realize that, despite being around people, I felt isolated. I craved time with friends my own age. I hadn't had my high school girlfriends around in a while and was looking forward to my baby shower, spending the day with the girls and having them ask me lots of questions only I could answer. Like "What's it feel like to be pregnant?" And "Are you scared to have the baby?" This made me feel special, and for the time helped me forget what was going on in real life.

I put on a beautiful, long red blouse with my black velvet stretchy pants, and it felt good to get dressed up. Kim, one of my oldest and dearest friends, hosted my lovely baby shower. There was a house full of young high school girls, my family, and Don's family, playing the usual games, talking about babies, and eating incredible little appetizers like ham-and-cheese wheels. The perfect way to celebrate the last few days of just being me.

In the middle of the night I woke to a horrible pain in my belly. It was time for my sweet baby boy to make his way into this world. As each contraction grew stronger, I was scared and uncertain of what was to come but I was also excited to know I would be holding my baby soon.

I moved from the bed to the couch, as sitting seemed to be better and relieved a little of the pressure. My mother and Don sat on the couch, helping me breathe through it and counting the minutes between contractions. After taking a few deep breaths, I relaxed for a brief moment, and just then, my water broke. I looked down to see my blue flannel nightgown soaked as the water ran down my mom's white leather couch. Donnie III was on his way, and it was time to get to the hospital.

We checked into St. Joe's, and I saw Don overjoyed as he waited for his first son to be born. Day turned into night and night turned into day. My body went through so much pain I didn't know what day it was anymore or how many hours I had been trying to have my baby. People kept coming and going while I did my best to stay calm and work through the pain. I was grateful to have my mother by my side, holding my hand.

After twenty-four hours of labor, my doctor finally came in to inform us that Donnie was a big baby and was not pushing with the crown of his head but with his forehead. I was in terrible pain by this time, and the doctor informed us that this was one of the most painful types of labors. Despite laboring for an entire day, I had dilated only two centimeters, so it was time for a C-section.

What? They were going to have to cut me open? All this time in labor was going to end in surgery? I was scared at the thought. But I just wanted a break and I needed those drugs I was trying so desperately to avoid.

The anesthesiologist entered and started prepping me. Don leaned over to say he thought the doctor had been drinking because he smelled like alcohol.

Really? You tell a teenage woman losing her mind with pain that the doctor getting ready to stick a gigantic needle into her spine might have been drinking? But before I knew it, I was being wheeled into the operating room, the nurses working quickly to prep me as the doctor started to cut. Suddenly, I panicked. Delirious from the pain, I tried to get up from the table to tell them I could feel everything. But after one shot of drugs to my IV, I hit the table.

I woke up to a very sore body and a stomach full of stitches, but all I could think about was holding Donnie. Moments later, the nurse laid him in my arms and I cradled my beautiful, sweet, strawberry-blond boy. I was a proud mommy no matter how old I was.

I had lots of visitors, everyone from Lisa and the crew of exotic dancers to my grandparents, and they all came bearing gifts. I had to stay in the hospital for a few days because of the C-section, and I got quite tired of Jell-O, instead longing for a Big Mac with fries. My parents showed up with my requested meal while Don was MIA, out celebrating somewhere.

Leaving the hospital was a huge turning point into adulthood. I arrived pregnant, but left as a mother, responsible for another person.

Arriving back at my parents' house, the three of us began to live as a family in my little room. My mother and dad were also helping my brother, Randy, raise his son. He had married his high school sweetheart, Jamie, who had been pregnant at the time. Not too long after Ryan was born, Jamie decided she wasn't ready to be a mother and left Ryan with my parents. Now both Randy and I were living at home with our babies.

Ryan and Donnie were ten months apart, so our house was busy. Mom worked hard to help take care of the kids, making bottles and changing diapers. I think in a lot of ways those two babies kick-started my mom's life again. She was created to be a mom and was really good at loving her children—maybe almost too good.

After Donnie's birth, I focused on preparing for graduation, which meant finishing up my classes and losing all the baby weight. I was exhausted, still learning the ropes of being a mother while simultaneously working hard to finish out my senior year with straight A's. I was staring at the finish line and needed to stay focused on the prize. I also wanted to avoid looking like a hot mess at graduation. I wanted to at least appear to have it all together, unashamed of the challenging year I had just experienced.

Graduation finally came, and my entire family attended. I stood there in my green-and-gold cap and gown, ready to accept my diploma with my friends. I looked up in the stands to see Don holding our handsome five-week-old son, Donnie. I had done it! I'd finished school *and* had my baby.

When I heard my name called, I stood with a renewed spirit of accomplishment. Stepping onto the stage and holding the diploma was such a great feeling. I hadn't given up and no one could take this away from me, not even Don.

Later, as the cameras flashed, I stood holding my diploma in one hand and my baby boy in the other, posing for pictures with all my best friends. I felt so proud to have made it through high school.

The excitement of graduation night quickly dissipated when Don decided to go out to a neighborhood party instead of celebrating with me.

My home life was beginning to implode as the quarters were tight and the personalities were clashing. My mom got tense whenever Don did something to Donnie she didn't approve of, like tickling him or teasing him.

I had to remind her that Don grew up as one of five children and this was his normal. Eventually words were exchanged and Don told me to pack my things, because we were leaving. It was late at night. But within a couple of hours, Don, the baby, and I were standing on his parents' doorstep in need of a place to sleep for the night.

Soon after, we found a place and were living in our own little apartment. It was small but bigger than my little bedroom at my parents' house. There was something exciting about having our first apartment. I loved having a Christmas tree of our own to decorate.

My parents dismissed their disagreements with Don and came over bearing gifts, like furniture and groceries. They wanted to be close to me and Donnie. But it was a bittersweet time, as Don began hitting the bars more frequently and I found myself spending more time with my parents, desperately in need of their help.

This became my life. I was eighteen years old and married to a man who was rarely around. We had no money, and I was stuck at home taking care of a baby while he went out to party. The illusion of a fairy-tale marriage was quickly wearing off, and the reality of what it was hit me hard.

I became somewhat of a recluse in this little apartment, spending my days at home with Donnie, watching soaps on TV, and imagining I was those characters. Pretty clothes, looking perfect, and having everyone love you—that's what I wanted. The desire to be needed was an addiction far greater than any drug, and it began eating me alive.

I was so often alone, I felt like I was losing my mind, wondering where my husband was and how he was spending his time.

One night, I was sitting in the parking lot of a topless bar, waiting for Don to come out. I had been out there for hours, thinking about what my life had come to. *How could he do this to me? What am I going to do? I love him, but how can he treat me like this?* I was the mother of his son. How could he be inside that bar, spending our money and watching other women dance? I just didn't understand.

The doors to the bar flew open and I saw Don, the man I loved, standing there happy and content.

Something happens to your self-worth when someone treats you like this. One minute he can't live without you and the next he can't even look at you. Every negative thought I'd ever had about myself flooded my mind. I was no good. I was damaged, flawed. No one else could ever want me or my child.

I didn't know how to exist like that anymore, so I decided to try to live more like Don. Maybe that would bring us closer together and we would be happy again. I hoped he would want to spend time with me instead of leaving me at home all the time. So I began to engage in the same things Don did, mainly drugs.

I wasn't much of a drinker, but I occasionally had just enough to take the edge off, allowing me to let go of my usual inhibitions. I thought maybe this would help me cope. Maybe he would behave differently. Maybe he would love me and treat me like a princess.

Cocaine became the drug of choice. I really didn't think much about doing drugs. It was just something to do to pass the time. Don didn't seem to think much of me, so why would I value myself? I became a party girl to Don, and this seemed to help our relationship a little. On many nights people came to our tiny apartment to party, and I thought, *At least he's home doing this.* It was a relief to me because I knew what was happening when he was there. I knew who he was with and I felt like at least I could somewhat control the other women he encountered. I had very little self-esteem, so it was easy to make these excuses work for me.

Many nights people I didn't know came in and out of our apartment to party, while I took Donnie and fell asleep in our bedroom.

Donnie was eighteen months old when Lisa and Mike came over with their little one, Mikey, to hang out for an evening full of alcohol and drugs. Just two couples getting together to hang out and get high all night while their kids ran around. The night continued on as if nothing really mattered until finally it was just Mike, Don, and me cutting lines on the glass coffee table into the early-morning hours.

When I'd had enough, I walked down the hall, passing Donnie's Mickey Mouse–clad bedroom, now dark and empty. I kept walking until I opened my bedroom door and there was Lisa, lying on my bed with Mikey on one side and Donnie on the other. The three of them sound asleep, looking so peaceful.

Even the drugs couldn't numb the self-hate I felt at that moment. How could I be doing cocaine in the other room while another woman put my son to bed as he snuggled up alongside her? What kind of mother was I? I had forgotten everything that was important to me.

A wave of emotions washed over me like nothing I'd felt before. I walked into the bathroom, shaking and struggling to breathe. It felt like I was having a heart attack, and in a way I was. Freaking out, crying, not sure what was going on, I caught my reflection in the mirror, and there was a dead woman looking back at me. Drugged and exhausted, I fell to my knees, crying out to a God I wasn't sure was there.

A broken voice came out. "Are you there, God? If You are, I need You. I need You." The drugs were destroying me and I had lost all self-respect. I knew my life needed to change, if not for myself, for my son. I sat on the floor for hours, crying, playing back my entire life in my head up until this sad, pathetic point, eventually falling asleep on the cold, hard bathroom floor.

Three days after the encounter with the dead woman in my bathroom, the phone rang and I was given a second chance. A man called, offering me my first modeling job. It came out of nowhere. As I hung up the phone, I looked at Don, who was cooking his cocaine in the kitchen. That was the first time I saw someone burn drugs on a stove. I took a long, hard look at Don and then disappeared into the living room. As I looked at my little Donnie, playing on the floor beside me, I had renewed hope and began to dream about my new life as a model.

5

Rock Star

❧

"Don't worry, girls. One day you'll find a guy
who ruins your lipstick, not your mascara."

JENNA MILNE

*Driving home, I lit a cigarette, rolled down the window, and
turned up the music, trying to drown out the awful truth of what
had just happened. Listening to Boston, I thought about my life
and how it felt like I was finally living my dream, only to see
it crushed right in front of me. I had been used, dismissed like
a groupie, and any ounce of confidence I had just gained was
extinguished like the cigarette I threw out the window. But as I
reached for another cigarette, I knew I too would be lit up again.
I just needed to figure out how.*

All I could think about was leaving for the Grand Cayman
Islands and having a chance to model. Things needed to
change in my life and my dream was finally coming true. I
was going to be a famous model. Now all I needed was the rock-
star boyfriend. I wanted those things so bad. I thought it could
make a difference, that it would make me successful and bring me
happiness. I needed to feel worthy in a world that put so much

importance on the opinions of strangers. Fame was the ultimate goal and I wanted some of it.

Grand Cayman was literally paradise. Warm and gorgeous, it felt good to be there all by myself, leaving my problems at home. I felt like I was finally coming into my own after being under someone's thumb for so long. I met the famous Bob Anderson, owner and creator of Ujena Swimwear and *Swimwear Illustrated* magazine. He made me feel like a superstar. He was kind and generous, which helped me feel like I belonged.

I was one of several women who had been flown in to model for the newest issue. Each one was tall, thin, tan, and absolutely gorgeous. They all seemed to be working models and acted like they knew everything about life and modeling. I was a little embarrassed sharing about how this was my first big shoot. I looked in awe at these beautiful women, reminded of how I had lost so much of myself and I didn't feel beautiful. I had so much doubt and insecurity. Nevertheless, I decided I would give it my best shot.

Every morning we got up early and headed down to the beach to begin the long day of shooting. The mornings were freezing cold and we were wearing next to nothing—swimwear, summer outfits, and bathing suit covers. Not a whole lot of fabric to keep a girl warm. We jumped into a large van and drove from location to location, trying to catch just the right light for the perfect shot.

It was a whole new world for me, and these women had such different life experiences from mine. While they talked about who they were dating, all I could think about was being married and having a baby while still being a child. Listening to these women share about traveling, shopping sprees, and wealthy men, I envied the lives they were living. One of the raven-haired beauties was dating a man who owned a vineyard in San Francisco. She talked about his huge mansion, decorated impeccably, where he threw lavish parties on the weekends. I thought, *She has the perfect life.* The guy might not be a rock star, but he was wealthy, and she was on her way to becoming a supermodel.

There was definitely a sense of jealousy among the girls, from who was going to make the cover, to what bathing suit someone wanted to wear in the shoot, to who had the attention of the photographers. I wanted to be noticed, to be seen as beautiful and successful, to have all the things these models had. One woman seemed to feel especially important, announcing to the rest of us that she was Bob's first choice and would be the one gracing the cover. Her words wounded me deeply.

When I finally made the cover of the next issue of the magazine, this woman let me know that it was the worst one ever. I'm not sure why I put such importance on her opinion, but I needed approval at the time, and she found a way to tear me down. Later I was able to put aside my feelings and let it go. I realized it didn't matter what she thought or how she treated me. The only thing that mattered was that I felt the weight of Don lifting off my shoulders and a new vision of my life coming to light.

The last night arrived, and it was bittersweet as I prepared to say good-bye to all my new friends and the glamorous life I had been living. As I was getting ready to go out, I was given a sexy two-piece skirt-and-top combo to wear out on the town. Each of the models got the same style in a different color to represent Ujena. The night was ours and we found ourselves in a restaurant bar playing loud music. We turned every head in the place as we sat down, ordering fluffy drinks and turtle. I was told it tastes like chicken, and they were right!

After eating, laughing, and feeling like a million bucks, it was time to get on the dance floor. We danced the night away and I was full of joy for the first time in forever.

The next morning I arrived at the airport, ready to return to real life. I had spent the last few weeks living a dream, and I stepped onto the plane with a spark of renewed confidence in myself. Flying back to Phoenix, all I could think about was continuing my modeling career, excited for the next time I would be posing for the camera.

I had butterflies in my stomach as I landed at the airport. I imagined Don, all cleaned up, standing there at the gate with Donnie, waiting for me as I got off the plane. But as I headed down the long corridor, I saw my parents with my sweet Donnie, huge smiles on their faces. Don did not come. My parents had been watching Donnie for a few days while he was working. I was disappointed, though not completely surprised, by this welcome home.

All the way home, my parents and I talked about my trip and all the incredible experiences I had, while I loved on Donnie. It was late when we arrived at my apartment, and I was still disappointed that Don hadn't cared enough to show up at the airport after I had been gone for a couple of weeks. But I was still on a high from working my dream job, so I tried to let it go.

My parents helped me with Donnie and my luggage, but when we walked up to the door, it was locked. I knocked several times while I looked for my key, but no one answered. I finally found it in my bag and opened the apartment door. A horrific smell hit me and I saw a complete mess. The kitchen sink was stacked high with dirty dishes, empty bottles of alcohol lay all over the floor, and stuff was scattered everywhere. I turned down the hallway and went into the bedroom to find piles of dirty clothes. I couldn't believe Don was not there. *Where was he?*

I looked around our room, and as I approached the bed, I found women's clothes that didn't belong to me lying on the floor. I couldn't believe what I was seeing. As I picked the clothing up off the floor, I knew it was time to make a decision. *Do I stay? Do I leave? Will he hurt me? Will he be happy to get rid of me?* The questions ran through my mind as tears streamed down my face.

I walked into Donnie's Mickey Mouse room, still as perfect

as the day I left. Obviously Donnie hadn't slept in his bed. Frustrated, confused, and hurt, I grabbed a suitcase, stuffed it with Donnie's and my clothes, and left with my parents, trembling all the way to their house. My mind was going crazy with questions. Full of anxiety, I had a hard time breathing.

Of course, the calls started rolling in from Don, full of hate one minute and love the next. I was confused and scared, but I now desired so much more for my life and Donnie's. I'd had a taste of success in the Grand Cayman Islands, and I did not want to go back to that broken relationship nor that trashy apartment.

Finally, Don and I agreed to separate. He continued telling me he was going to get clean, change his ways, and be a standup husband and father. He didn't want to lose us. But I couldn't go back until I knew he had changed. I moved back in with my parents and started to find a new life.

Moving forward, I wanted to spend more time among friends. One in particular. Noel had married a drummer, and his band happened to be playing nearby, so she invited me to come hang out for the night. It was the '90s and big hair was in, so I put on the coolest rock 'n' roll outfit I owned—black stretch pants and a bolero jacket with white appliqués. I had seen the lead female singer of Roxette wearing something similar in her music video, "Dangerous." I'd just gotten a perm, so my hair was crazy curly and my makeup was bold. I was ready to hit the club.

I walked in feeling confident, and I think everyone noticed. Noel had a table close to the stage and was sitting there, waiting for me. I had butterflies in my stomach, thinking about my life. I had just come off a modeling shoot and now here I was sitting front row as a special guest of the band. It didn't matter that they were the local entertainment, because that night they were the "it" band.

The bar got dark, the lights came up on the stage, and there they were, rock gods dancing around in their skin-tight leather pants, long hair, and black eyeliner. I was living the dream!

A couple of songs in, Noel and a few of the other girls got up to dance and I joined them. I ended up right in front of the tall, tan, muscular blond playing lead guitar and singing backup. I flashed him a big smile and batted my wing-lined eyes at him. I knew nothing about him, except that his name was Ben, but I was sold since he was a rock star.

I went home that night in a trance. My dream was right in front of me! As I climbed into bed, my head was filled with beautiful thoughts of my future as a model with a rock-star boyfriend by my side.

A couple of weeks passed and I couldn't stop thinking about that night at the club. Ben and I spent many nights having conversations that lasted for hours, getting to know each other.

One night my phone rang, and it was Noel, inviting me to her home for a party with some friends. My first question was "Will Ben be there?" Though we'd talked on the phone, we hadn't seen each other since our first encounter at the bar.

"Yep, he will," she responded.

I arrived at the party excited to see Ben. Seeing him for only the second time, after hours of talking on the phone, I felt like a schoolgirl with a crush, butterflies and all.

We were all enjoying ourselves, talking and having drinks, when halfway into the party I heard someone outside screaming and knocking over garbage cans. I looked out the window and saw Don, out of control and threatening everyone.

Eventually he left, and Noel asked me to leave too. She and the rest of her guests were worried about Don, and I didn't blame them. I said my good-byes to Ben and walked to my car, my head hung low, looking over my shoulder to make sure Don wasn't lurking in the shadows. When I got in my car, I cranked up the music. Tears streamed down my face as I headed home.

A few days later, I found out Don had heard from someone that Ben and I had connected. Don threatened Ben and me, but that didn't stop our relationship from moving forward. We continued to have long hours of conversation, and I couldn't help but fall in love with the handsome rock star. He seemed like everything I wanted in a guy. He knew all the right words to say. We'd had more phone conversations than in-person meetings, but that was fine with me. He was busy with his job and the band, and I was raising Donnie while working. Ben was living with his sister at the time, so when I did see him, I often spent the evening there with him and his family.

I had recently picked up a second job for a fashion-show wholesale company, working as a floor model. My colleagues and I went to restaurants and bars and put on fashion shows, where customers bid on the beautiful clothes we wore. It was as close as I'd gotten to being a model.

I became good friends with the family who owned the company. I would sit for hours with Jan, the owner, talking about life and smoking cigarettes. I loved her and all the people I worked with.

Don stayed away during this time, but he wasn't doing anything to clean up his act. I tried to pull money together for our divorce and to pay off our debts. Credit companies called me daily, asking for payment, since I was the only one working. Don quit his job because he didn't want to pay child support or any of the debt he'd racked up over the previous couple of years. Even though the situation was awful, I tried to stay positive and look on the bright side. I had a beautiful baby boy, I was working as a model, and I was dating a handsome rock star.

Just as I started falling hard for Ben, a crushing blow came. I found out he had been lying to me since the day I met him. He had a girlfriend—and not just a casual relationship. They had been living together for years. I couldn't believe he had been deceiving me. But when I thought about it, so many things started to make sense. We rarely saw each other in person, and when we did, it was always at his sister's place. When I saw him at the bars he performed at, he kept me at arm's length, saying he feared Don, which wasn't hard to believe.

I was outraged at the lies and how I'd allowed myself to believe in this man. I thought, *Is every man a liar? Are all men just out to use women?* I couldn't believe his sister had lied to me too. In fact, his entire family had. *Am I in some kind of crazy movie? Why would people do such a thing to someone like me?*

I drove to his sister's house, where he told me he lived, and knocked on the door. His sister finally answered. Ben must have warned her I was on my way, since I could see the distress on her face. I told her I wanted to see Ben. Tammy walked to the wall phone and dialed. She and Ben spoke for a few minutes, then she handed me the phone. Apparently, Kelly, his girlfriend, was sitting next to him. He told me it was over between us, that he had made a mistake and was staying with her.

I was crushed. His tone made it sound like I was a groupie he couldn't get rid of. Although he was undoubtedly putting on a front for her, it still hurt like crazy.

Tammy stood nearby, looking on. I hung up and she tried to explain why she had gone along with the deception. Tammy didn't like Kelly, nor did his family, and they were hopeful Ben would leave her and start fresh with me. It was nice to hear they felt that way about me, but it didn't make up for the fact I had been played by Ben and his entire family.

I left in complete disbelief of what had just happened. I had tried so hard to be part of this dream world and find some happiness. But all my hopes were crushed.

6

Ladies Don't Smoke

⊱─◦─⊰

"The only thing worse than a boy that hates you:
a boy that loves you."

Markus Zusak, *The Book Thief*

I started my day with coffee in hand, in the smoke-filled room full of pretty clothes. My boss walked in, carrying a vase full of long-stemmed red roses. She stopped right in front of me and handed me the beautiful bouquet. Surprised and slightly confused, I reached for the card and opened it. I took a long drag off my cigarette as I carefully read the note. It made me so angry. All I could think was, Why would a man do something like this?

How do you forget that your heart has been broken? You head to the most magical place on earth: Disneyland. My parents knew how pained I was over Ben, and they wanted me to forget about everything and just enjoy myself. I needed some time to think, to process all that I'd gone through with yet another man, without the distractions of everyday life.

I wasn't sure that I was in love with Ben, but I was definitely enamored by the idea of him. Who doesn't fall head over heels for a good-looking guy with a guitar singing on stage? I'd dreamt of marrying a rock star, and he was just that.

We often want what we can't have, and being on the receiving end of the break-up talk made my heart feel more broken than it was.

But how do we know what love is? Is it the feeling of needing a person? Believing you can't be without him? Is it physical—an electric feeling you get when the two of you touch? I don't think we know what love is until we actually experience it. So I just kept guessing.

Before my family and I left for our trip to California, my friend Julie called me about her brother, Stephen. We had all gone to high school together. Stephen was a senior when Julie and I were freshmen. He was very handsome, blond, and he'd played in the high school band. I remembered his striking smile as we passed by each other in the hallways of the school. Julie told me that Stephen had recently broken up with his girlfriend and she wanted to know if it was okay for him to call me. I told her I was heading to California but would love to talk with him when I returned.

My family packed up the car and headed to Disneyland. The road trip allowed me to forget all the adult problems I was dealing with at home and just enjoy spending time with Donnie and my parents, living like a princess while eating cotton candy until I got sick. As we made our way through "It's a Small World" and "Pirates of the Caribbean," I felt like just as much of a child as Donnie was. We held each other's hands and giggled like best friends.

Returning from California, refreshed and ready to jump back into ordinary life, I was thrilled to see a message on the answering machine from Stephen. He invited me to a sporting event with his family, and it turned out I could go. I was used to always having a guy in my life, and there was a part of me that didn't feel complete without one by my side. I hoped, *Maybe Stephen would be that new guy*. I didn't want to be alone, and having someone to go out with helped Band-Aid what had happened with Ben.

Meanwhile, Don was still "working" on himself, or so he said. He had gone through a thirty-day rehab program; however, the day he was released, he went to bars with his brothers. He blamed me for that because I hadn't been at the rehab clinic to pick him up. Just another excuse to shirk responsibility for his behavior and addictions.

He jumped right back into going to bars and dating topless dancers. I would've been fine with that if he'd just continued to live his own life, but instead he kept trying to control mine. We had horrible fights over the phone about him wanting to see Donnie. He threw out threats that made me want to avoid him altogether.

Before my date with Stephen, Don and I had a particularly violent conversation. When I mentioned I wasn't dating Ben anymore, Don's tone changed to one I hadn't heard in forever. It was almost sweet yet completely toxic. I knew he thought he had scared Ben into breaking up with me. I was just glad he didn't know the truth, that Ben dumped me for his live-in girlfriend. The last thing I wanted was one crazy maniac telling me "I told you so" about another crazy maniac.

There were times when my heart tried to convince me that maybe, just maybe, Don would change. But as I finished getting ready to go out one night, my mind went back to the night I arrived home late from work and realized I didn't have my key to get into the apartment Don and I shared. The lights were on, so I knocked on the door for a few minutes, but there was no answer. I crawled through some bushes that circled the small patio off of our apartment kitchen. I looked through the tiny opening of the vertical blinds, and there on the floor of the walkway, right next to the front door, was Don, with Donnie in his diaper next to him, both asleep. *How did Don not hear me knock?* I made my way back to the front door, knocked louder, and rang the doorbell. No answer, but Donnie started crying. I rushed back to the sliding door so I could see what was going on. Don was still passed out, with Donnie screaming next to him. I got scared, thinking something might be wrong with Don. *Is he unconscious? Dead? What has he been doing while he's supposed to be taking care of our baby?*

Panicked, I went to my landlord's place to get a master key. I was reeling out of control, losing my mind with thoughts of all the things that could've taken place. Arriving back at the apartment, I opened the door and there stood Don. I grabbed Donnie out of his arms right away. Don started to explain that he had been doing drugs, started drinking, then passed out with Donnie. I was livid.

I did my best to shake the bad memory of that night and finish getting ready for my date.

Stephen came to the door and my mother answered it, welcoming him in. I came around the corner and saw him standing there, tall and trim, with beautiful blond hair tousled like he had just walked off the beach. He gave me that same striking smile I remembered from seeing him in the hallways at high school.

We jumped into his big white truck with a bench seat. His truck was spotless, since he was a very clean and organized person, which I appreciated. The entire evening was so easy, as if no time had passed. We were two friends reconnecting after years apart. I didn't worry about impressing him or acting like I was something I wasn't. The night ended with a friendly hug and a kiss on the cheek.

I felt so grown-up, going on a date with a man and having him walk me to the door. This was new to me. *Could this relationship blossom into something else? Can I really fall for the brother of one of my good friends?* When I lay my head down that night, questions flooded my mind. *Will Don and his crazy jealousy cause problems for me again? Will Stephen hurt me the way Ben did?* Then images of Stephen's smile, his carefree ways, and the wonderful evening we'd shared ran through my head. I felt at peace as I went to sleep.

Stephen called me a couple of days after our first date. I was excited to hear his voice. He asked if I'd like to come over for dinner. I was thrilled that he was going to cook for me. Stephen's condo was about ten minutes from my parents' place. The proximity made it easy for us to reconnect.

I decided to put a little more effort into getting ready for this second date. I slipped on a white bodysuit and my tight, high-waisted jeans. I ratted my hair out, completing the look with brick-brown lipstick.

I could tell my mother was excited for me. She couldn't stop talking about how good-looking Stephen was and about his wavy blond hair. I hugged her and kissed Donnie good-bye for the evening.

After jumping into my red Fiero, I headed over to Stephen's place. I pulled into his charming complex full of trees, with each unit having its own parking space. I drove all the way around to the back to his condo and found him standing outside, waiting for me.

There was something very natural about the relationship as he greeted me with that smile and a hug, then showed me into his place. I was impressed by how clean and beautifully decorated it was, with a small dining table set for two in the corner. He had dinner cooking on the stove, a homemade sauce that had been simmering all afternoon and smelled delicious. He poured me a glass of wine and showed me around his place, then we sat down for a special Italian dinner. We chatted, catching up on the past—what we had done after high school, our relationships, our mutual love of music, our jobs, and my life as a single mom.

As I held my glass of wine, smiling and feeling warm all over, it wasn't hard to imagine myself dating Stephen. By the looks of his place, he seemed like he had it all together, and what he was saying sounded perfect.

We ended up on the couch and I experienced my first real kiss with him. There was something about that kiss that didn't call out love but evoked a passionate, sexual feeling in me. I knew right then it was time for me to leave and get home to Donnie.

I drove home with my mind racing, thinking about that kiss. I hadn't experienced that level of passion before. I couldn't put my finger on what was different about it. I replayed the kiss over and over in my head, the feeling burning deep inside of me.

Stephen and I started seeing each other more and more. We spent a lot of time at his place or with his friends because I wasn't twenty-one yet. I had a fake ID, but it had been taken away from me at a nightclub I'd wanted to dance at with my girlfriends.

It was only a couple of months before my birthday, so I was content to just sit on the couch and watch TV with Stephen. We were still getting to know each other. I made sure Stephen and Donnie spent time together too. He was kind to Donnie, but he just wasn't ready for, or interested in, being a dad.

The group I did fashion shows with was heading up north on a camping trip for the weekend, and there was talk about shooting photos up by the waterfalls. I really wanted to go. I asked Stephen to join me and he said yes. I was excited to show him off to the girls. I was also eager to spend the weekend alone with him and introduce him to my world.

We drove up north in his big white truck and arrived on the

site of the campgrounds, which was lined with tall, green trees and running streams. As we put up the tent, I realized we would be sleeping together in the same tent, though in separate sleeping bags. I was more worried about what I would look like in the morning than being intimate with him.

We set up camp, then threw on our bathing suits and headed for the waterfalls, with the Arizona sun blazing above. The other models and I climbed up the rocks, striking supermodel poses. I pulled out all the stops, knowing Stephen was watching me. I hoped he would see me as beautiful on the outside and wouldn't notice how damaged I was on the inside.

After a long day of laughing and flirting, Stephen and I made our way back to the campground. As we sat around the campfire, sharing stories and listening to Stephen play his guitar while we sang, my feelings for him grew even stronger.

The evening wound down and we headed to the tent. We crawled in together, both feeling a little awkward. Then the kiss happened and everything changed.

By the end of the trip, our relationship had moved to the next level and it was official—I was his girlfriend.

I started staying at Stephen's place more than my parents' house, allowing me lots of freedom and a chance for our relationship to grow.

With Stephen I had felt a feeling I had never experienced before. I felt desired. I had been with other men, but those relationships never had the same electricity. They almost felt like addictions. I mistook the sensuality and sex in those relationships as love. It felt so good to be with Stephen I thought, *This must be what it looks like to be in love, and to have someone love you. How could it not be?*

My twenty-first birthday approached, and I had the entire night planned, hanging out with the girls then connecting with

Stephen to continue celebrating. My girlfriends took me to a place with very tan male dancers, who pulled me onto the stage and gave me a lap dance. It creeped me out, and I was shocked to see how many women they were kissing. When a dancer came in to give me a birthday kiss, I gave him the cheek and ducked out of my time on stage.

As I returned to the table, strawberry daiquiri in hand, my girlfriends toasted this newly christened twenty-one-year old. I was enjoying my cocktail when I looked up and saw a tall, handsome rocker with long hair and leather pants standing at the end of my table. It was Ben. He hadn't been invited to my birthday party! But his band was playing after the male dancers.

Before I got two words out of my mouth, Stephen appeared at the table next to him. So awkward! I introduced them to each other. Stephen knew who Ben was and what he'd done to me, but he didn't react negatively. That was something I appreciated about my new go-with-the-flow boyfriend. The two guys shook hands, and that was that.

Stephen and I quickly took off, moving on to the next club to continue the celebration. While walking up to the next club, a little hole-in-the-wall place with a packed parking lot, all I could think about was being legal. No club could keep me out now.

The doors flew open, and there was the band—Chuck Hall and the Brick Wall—playing music that shook the building and everyone inside of it. Stephen and I headed straight for the bar, ordered the usual Gentleman Jack and Coke, then danced the night away to the bluegrass music.

It was a magical night, but it came and went like any other. I was hoping for some big change to happen to me after I turned twenty-one. I kept thinking there was something else out there for me. I barely made ends meet, yet I was dying to have a place of my own. That wasn't going to happen with the money I made working the fashion shows. I had been promoted from model to emcee, and I loved getting to dress up and engage the crowd.

Stephen and I were in a pretty serious, committed relationship, hopefully on our way to marriage. I believed that one day he would get on his knee, throw his beautiful blond hair back, flash me that striking smile, and profess his love for me by putting a sparkly ring on my finger.

Dreaming of this special moment, I started off my workday one morning with coffee in hand, walking through the smoke-filled room full of pretty clothes. My boss walked in, carrying a bouquet of flowers. I thought it was sweet of her husband to do that. But she proceeded to hand them to me. Confused, I reached for the card and saw they were from Ben. He said he wanted me to know he was still in love with me. *What?* Wasn't he preparing to walk down the aisle with the blonde bombshell he'd kept secret from me? Why was he sending me flowers and telling me he loved me?

I was so angry a man would do something like that. I lit a cigarette, sat down, and played our entire relationship back in my head. But my subconscious, the one that had been dreaming of dating a rock star since childhood, kept pulling up images of this talented musician, standing on stage with leather pants and long blond hair, strumming an electric guitar and singing "Some Kind of Wonderful."

Stop it! Just stop it! I thought. *Smoke another cigarette and don't even think about calling him.* I was done with the rock star, and I was moving on with my laid-back hippie.

Part Three

THE CAGED CANARY

Finding Myself

The bird goes *tweet, tweet, tweet*. Silly bird!

Sitting at lunch, my mom and I reminisced about my childhood in Cooperstown. There were many sweet memories, but one stood out in my mind. We'd had a pet, a little blue-and-white canary by the name of Blue Boy. Just thinking of him made me grin from ear to ear. I laughed out loud as I retold a story of this little bird's gallant efforts.

This persistent little canary always found a way out of his cage. He would fly to the top of the stairs and then, with his little stick-like legs and sharp nails, he would begin the descent to the bottom of the carpeted staircase. He usually made it down at least ten steps before his journey came to an abrupt end. When he got to the last step, he'd get caught and ended up hanging upside down!

Now, you'd think that after the first time of getting snagged in the carpeting, Blue Boy would just fly to the bottom of the stairs and make his escape. But he didn't. Many times we found him hanging upside down, with one foot stuck in the carpet, just chirping away, waiting for someone to come to his rescue.

How many of us walk through life like that little bird? We work hard to get out of the cage, then hop down the long staircase of life, and just as we catch a glimpse of the bottom, our foot gets caught and we find ourselves hanging upside down! We think, *What am I going to do? How did I get here? I was so close. Can anyone hear me? Does anyone even care?*

Silly birds we are! How many times must we walk that same set of stairs only to get caught up in the carpet? We must make changes in our strategy in order to complete our journey. Maybe there is a better way to get to that destination, without finding ourselves hanging upside down. Or maybe we should be using those wings God gave us to fly.

7

Of Two Minds

＞•◈•◯•◈•＜

"Love looks not with the eyes,
but with the mind, And therefore
is winged Cupid painted blind."

WILLIAM SHAKESPEARE,
A MIDSUMMER NIGHT'S DREAM

There I stood in my beautiful ivory dress, looking down the long aisle at the man who was standing there, waiting for me to become his. My parents had refused to give me their blessing, but despite feeling hurt, I had convinced myself that I'd found the one I wanted to marry. As I took a few steps into that church filled with people, I was suddenly overcome with anxiety. Was I doing the right thing? Was this man the one I wanted to spend the rest of my life with?

Blinded by love, I had created this fantasy life with Stephen. Our relationship seemed nothing like my previous ones and I felt different about him, longing to be with him every waking moment. We would lie together on the couch, listening to "Evergreen," a song that spoke about the love we shared. I hoped our relationship would always be easy, fresh, and certain. I felt secure in his arms, looking up at his smile, believing we were on our way to marriage, ageless and forever.

But my seemingly flawless love affair was about to take a turn. One night, I excitedly made dinner for the two of us at his apartment. I cooked, set the table, lit the candles, and put on soft music, then waited for him to walk through the door. I waited and waited. The candles burned down, my dinner became dry and overcooked, and I had played every song on the CD. I moved from the couch to the dining room table, then eventually to bed. Hours went by and the reality finally hit—he wasn't coming back.

Around midnight I got in my car to go home, running through a whole list of possible reasons he hadn't come back for dinner to spend an evening with the woman he loved. *Where was he? Was he okay? Did something come up?* All my insecurities from when I was with Don came flooding back, invading my mind.

The next day I woke, desperate to know what happened. I called Stephen, but there was no answer. I went to his apartment, but he was already gone, or maybe he had never come home. I called him at work and was told he would call me back later. When Stephen and I finally spoke, he told me he had spontaneously decided to hang out with friends that night and basically forgot about our dinner plans. He acted like it didn't have anything to do with me. Believing he would never do anything to purposefully hurt me, I made it all okay in my mind and moved on.

Stephen was young and still flying like a free bird. I should have realized he wasn't ready to settle down, but for some reason I still held on to the hope that he would marry me. Our relationship was sexual and dysfunctional, but still seemed better than the last one. I wanted so badly to love, to be loved, and to have a father for Donnie, I could only see what I wanted to see, blind to everything else.

But as our relationship continued, so did the all-nighters.

Stephen seemed much more interested in his friends, topless bars, and blues clubs than dating me and helping me raise my son. My history was hitting me right in the face. He was doing the same thing to me that Don had.

There is only so much a woman can take before completely losing her identity and self-worth. But just as I would reach a low, the next night I found myself singing karaoke with Stephen, Jack and Coke in hand, belting out "I Got You, Babe," in a dive bar. Suddenly everything bad he had done the previous week melted away like the ice in my drink, and he hooked me back in with his sweet, intoxicating kisses. I filled up my glass, fixed my lipstick, and sang "These Boots Are Made for Walking." Up on that stage, with a drink in one hand and a cigarette in the other, I felt like a rock star. I could mask any insecurities with a strong take-charge song, making everyone in the room believe I was confident and together.

The night of singing ended in a drunken stupor, and I found myself back at Stephen's place. After a night full of laughter and passion, I woke up next to him, in love all over again. I drove home dreaming of the day he would ask me to marry him. And the vicious cycle would start again.

Like a rose under the April snow, our relationship was more like a frozen grave than a growing love. I thought maybe this was just the way love was supposed to be. My self-esteem dropped and my neediness grew. I was tired of the lonely nights and the excuses that always followed them. "Why did you do this?" became "How could you do this to me again?" As the fighting escalated, my hope of having an everlasting love faded away.

Stephen and I had been dating for almost two years when I found myself desperate. Another Friday night rolled around and he told me he would be going out with his friends for a few drinks after the long week of work. I knew this meant I would not see him all night, so I jumped into my car and drove to one of his normal hangouts. I sat in my car, glaring at his white pickup truck parked in front of a topless bar, exactly where I thought he would be. As the music played on the radio, I couldn't stop thinking about how this male behavior was becoming my normal, and that I was allowing this to happen to me. I touched up my makeup, threw my purse over my shoulder, and headed for the door.

I got up to the front, flashed my ID, and entered the topless bar. Every eye turned as I walked through that door, the light shining behind me. For a split second I thought maybe the men were checking me out. Then I realized they were trying to see whose wife or girlfriend had just walked in.

After my eyes adjusted, I spotted Stephen by the stage toward the back. I stopped at the bar and ordered a cocktail. I wasn't sure what I was going to say, but I figured the drink would help. I walked toward the stage, watching Stephen's every move. How many dollars he was spending and which dancers he was interested in. "She's My Cherry Pie" came on, and so did a long-legged brunette, strutting down the runway, shaking everything she had. She was perfect from head to toe, and I knew it would be impossible to get my man's attention.

I noticed the bouncer keeping an eye on me. They were probably trained to watch the women who entered since many of them came in looking for someone, hell bent on starting a fight. I took a seat at Stephen's table, trying to keep my cool so I didn't get myself thrown out.

One word led to another and the tears started to flow. Stephen was irate. He couldn't believe I had the audacity to follow him to this bar and confront him inside.

As he talked, I kept thinking about my ex-husband, Don, and his love for this type of place, and the women he ended up with. Then my thoughts went on to Ben, who dumped me for his live-in girlfriend. I had to leave immediately, to get out of this place, with or without Stephen.

Comfort. It's what we all want in our lives. But oftentimes comfort is not a good thing. It breeds a sense of false security. We stop moving, stop changing, stop growing. Instead we stand still, afraid of what could be and convincing ourselves this is the best it will ever be. Or at least, it's better to know than to take a chance. It takes a lot of faith, and a lot of trust, to break out of our comfort zone and step into the unknown.

I thought what I had with Stephen was love, but really I was just comfortable and afraid to be alone.

It seemed the only real love in my life was Donnie. I tried my best to be a good mom, bending over backward to save money and look after my son. None of which I was good at. I was just a broken little girl. Thank God for my parents. They were the only solid rock in my life. My family was the one place where I knew I was loved.

Meanwhile, totally dysfunctional romantic relationships became normal for me. So I made myself more seductive and focused on being the "lady in waiting" instead of the desperate girlfriend who would follow her man and try to make waves.

I decided it was time for Donnie and I to have our own place. I was working odd jobs to make ends meet, hostessing at The Big Apple, which later turned into waitressing, and sewing on my off times to make extra money. I'd grown up with a grandma and a great-grandma who were both seamstresses, and they taught me to make Barbie doll clothes at an early age. Barbie doll clothes soon turned into pillows that turned into window coverings, and eventually I started making swimming suits. It was hard work, but I needed the money.

One day I was out running errands when I ran into Lisa, Mike's ex-girlfriend. We had a quick catch-up session standing in the grocery aisle. I shared what I was doing with my life, and she shared about going back to dancing to make ends meet for her and Mikey. She was working at a new topless bar not far from where I lived. As we ended our conversation, she said, "Well, if you're making bathing suits, do you think you could make dancer's costumes?"

She went on to tell me how the dancers had to buy new costumes on a regular basis and they paid hundreds of dollars for them. Any hesitation I had was quickly eliminated by the dollar signs running through my mind.

I drove around thinking of all the possibilities of this new business venture. As soon as I got home, I called my mom. I told her about running into Lisa at the grocery store, and I shared with her about my idea for a prosperous entrepreneurship that could bring in extra money for me and Donnie. I told her I'd worked out in my mind what I needed to get into business making exotic dancers' costumes. I was excited about this legitimate, lucrative, perfect idea.

My mother listened in silence, then encouraged me to give it a try. My parents stepped in and helped me put together my small business.

We all need money, and at times we find ourselves doing things we wouldn't normally do to get it. There I was, coming up with a business plan that revolved around the profession I despised in so many ways because the women involved in it captivated the men I had been in relationships with. But I needed to make ends meet to live and feed my child. It seems that everyone has a price.

As I got to know the business, I also got to know the women, and most of them had a heartbreaking story. They had not chosen this lifestyle, but they needed the money, just like I did, to survive. For most of them, this was all they knew, and they had no self-worth or drive to try to achieve anything more.

Of Two Minds

I convinced my parents to help me purchase a special sewing machine that would make it possible for me to make these costumes with greater speed while dealing with delicate fabrics my normal machine couldn't handle. I sat for hours designing a costume, picking the material, creating a pattern, cutting it out, and then sewing it together. Afterward I spent hours meticulously putting on rhinestones or hand-painting the fabric, whatever it took to make them gorgeous. Despite all the time and effort, I believed this was the answer to all my monetary needs.

When I had finished a few costumes, I felt ready to go out and see if I could sell them. I wanted to be taken seriously, so I got all dressed up in tight jeans, spiked heels, and perfect hair, thinking I needed to look the part. I headed to the exotic dancers' club Lisa worked at. I pulled up to the bar and sat in my car for some time, thinking about what I was getting ready to do. I lit a cigarette and thought about what I would say and how much I would charge. I had it all planned out in my head. Now all I had to do was go and do it.

Taking a deep breath like my life depended on it, I got out of the car and walked toward the door, where two huge bouncers stood like warriors, watching me. They were on high alert, making sure I wasn't coming in to start trouble. I was shaking in my stilettos, but I kept going…until the bouncer stopped me and asked me what I was doing there and what was in the bag. I felt like a little kid who had just gotten in trouble. After I spilled my guts, he told me to wait for a minute, then went inside to get Lisa. She came out and vouched for me.

Lisa seemed excited to see me. She led me into the dark, smoke-filled bar, with loud music and a smell I could never forget. Cigarette smoke and booze filled the air. I followed Lisa through the bar, past the beautiful women dancing on a dimly lit stage while salacious men sat there, captivated by their every move. I felt like I was in slow motion, and that every eye was watching me as I walked by.

Lisa took me into the back dressing room, where all the dancers were touching up their makeup, making costume changes, or smoking cigarettes while resting their feet after dancing around in five-inch stilettos. A costume lady was already there, showing off her designs to the girls. I set my bag down, and instead of pulling out my costumes, I got out a cigarette and waited for Lisa to introduce me to the other dancers. I felt a little out of place, but tried to act like someone who knew what was going on. I needed to fit in, because most of these women were rough around the edges and this would only work if they thought I was one of them.

After the costume designer left, it was my turn. I stood up with knees shaking, holding my little plastic bag, as Lisa introduced me as one of her good friends. I was in! If I was a friend to Lisa then I was a friend to them. Instantly I had gained their trust because they trusted her. Within a few minutes I had most of the dancers coming over to see what I had created. Several of them asked if I could customize the costumes, make them in different colors and sizes. I sold everything I had made and took orders for several more. I left the bar with two thing on my mind: making more costumes and making lots of money.

I worked around the clock sewing, and eventually gave up my waitressing job at The Big Apple. I was getting sucked into it as I made friends and money both at the same time. I loved having money and being able to provide for my son.

I started driving from club to club late at night, waiting until just the right time. Knowing how the shift changes worked, I wanted to make sure the ladies had time to work a bit first to make some money. Money in their hand meant money in my pocket.

My relationship with Stephen wasn't getting any better. It was really only about one thing, and that seemed to be getting old. I sought out some old friends and looked for different things to do on my nights off.

One night I received a call from an old friend who invited me out for the evening to go dancing at a club. I got all dressed up, then jumped in my car and headed out for the night. As I stood in front of the window to pay to get in, a familiar voice from behind me said hello. I took a deep breath and turned around to find myself standing face-to-face with Ben. He was clad in leather pants and a ripped-up T-shirt, his body tan and his blond hair in all its rock-god glory.

For a moment the world around me paused. Ben sounded really excited to see me, and I was trying to hide my excitement. He asked me if I was there to see his band play, and I was totally confused. "No," I responded, "I'm here to meet Nancy and some girls to hang out for an evening of dancing." I suddenly realized that Nancy's husband and his band were playing with Ben.

I asked where his wife was and he told me he was getting a divorce and was back to living with his parents.

I was completely flustered by this unexpected encounter and the things Ben was saying. The memories of us dating and the lies that he told flew through my mind. I couldn't believe this was happening. I was dating Stephen, and here I was at a bar where my ex-boyfriend's band was playing.

I escaped to the bar, hoping a cocktail might ease me into reality. My conscience told me to leave, but for some reason I couldn't.

When the last song was announced, it was "She's Some Kind of Wonderful." Did Ben do this on purpose? My eyes were locked on him. I watched every move he made, every smile that came across his face, every toss of his hair. The music took over and I couldn't stop thinking that just maybe we had come back together for a reason. I was right back where I started with Ben, and suddenly my dream of marrying a rock star returned.

The next morning, a loud knock on my apartment door made my stomach drop. I fixed my hair and then opened the door to see Ben standing there, holding flowers. They were beautiful!

Ben invited me on a date. I accepted, then lied to Stephen about my plans for that night, so I could see what, if anything, I still felt for Ben. He took me on a real date and it was nice to be out with him, feeling like he actually wanted to spend time with me instead of hiding in the shadows of a strip bar. However, now I was the one hiding in the shadows and not wanting to be found out.

We went back to my place, and Ben and I stayed up all night, talking about what we had been doing, how our relationships were going, and of course why his came to an end. That night he professed his love for me and said that he had never stopped thinking of me. He was so sorry for everything he had done. He said he was ready to commit to me the day he sent me the roses, but he understood why I hadn't responded. When I didn't respond, he went through with the wedding.

Soon after my reunion with Ben, Stephen and I ended our relationship. My lease was up on my apartment and Ben was moving at high speed, asking me to move in with him. Before I knew it, I was moving Donnie and myself into his parents' old house and helping him remodel it, believing we would get married and live happily ever after.

I was happy with Ben, and it seemed I was finally getting what I really wanted. I had someone who loved me and wanted to be with Donnie and me. I started making a home for the three of us, as this sweet romance blossomed…the romance that should have happened the first time around. Ben was playing in his band and doing really well. Friday and Saturday nights were dedicated to his music, and Ben was quick to reassure me Don was no longer a threat to him and he would never let me go again.

Ben planned a night out for the two of us, so we got all dressed up and went out for a nice dinner. We sat across from each other, talking about how this should have happened two years prior. Ben again professed his love for me, and with the last "I love you" and "I'm sorry for all that I've done," he pulled out a beautiful box and opened it to reveal an incredible sparkly ring. It had a gorgeous diamond with a triangular sapphire on each side. It was breathtaking and I was ecstatic as he slid it onto my finger and asked me to be his wife.

We began planning our wedding, and Ben's family was excited for us, helping make all the preparations. However, my parents were anything but thrilled about this marriage. They did not believe I was doing the right thing for Donnie or myself and would not give me their blessings. I was hurt. But head over heels in love, I couldn't see past the hazy fog of my emotions.

My 1940s ivory gown was beautiful, adorned with little diamond buttons, making me feel as unique as the dress. I made my way up to the front of the church, trying to escape the swirling thoughts in my head. As the pastor said the last words, announcing Ben and me as husband and wife, a sinking feeling hit me like a punch to the gut. I took a deep breath and shook it off.

As Ben and I walked back down the aisle, I looked around at all the rock stars sitting in the church with their bombshells next to them. I smiled and felt comforted, knowing that now I too was one of them.

8

Magic Man

>-+>-0-<+-<

"My head screamed no.
My heart whispered yes. Reality told me not to,
but hope told me to give it a shot."

MARILYN MONROE

There I was, sitting on the cold floor of the bathroom, waiting for the results of my test. I had finished school and gotten a job, and life finally seemed to be coming together for me. Minutes felt like hours as I waited to see what would determine my fate. I knew my future would come down to this very moment.

After partying all night long with the band, I sat in front of my vanity, staring at my makeup smudged under my eyes, a far cry from the modeling pictures that lined Ben's walls. The room was dark, and as I turned around, looking past the piles of clothes lying everywhere, I caught a glimpse of Ben asleep in bed. All I'd dreamt about was living like a rock star, but in reality, it was starting to get old, and unfortunately, so was my marriage to Ben. I thought he would bring me happiness, but the magic had quickly faded when the money got tight. Ben needed to make some decisions about his future, and I couldn't stop thinking about Stephen, wondering if I had made the right choice.

Indecision breeds discontent, and I found it impossible to be truly happy. I was craving consistency in love and in life, yet whenever things got too hard, I needed something new to feel any sort of hope. It was a cycle I couldn't get out of, and I found myself wishing I could go back and change the past.

I was working around the house one day when KC, Ben's ex-wife's brother, came to visit. Ben wasn't home yet, so he decided to wait. I invited him in and we started making small talk. KC mentioned how happy he was that Ben and his sister had made amends and that they were talking again. This was news to me, since Ben had never mentioned it. I tried to hide the fact that I was in complete shock by smiling and nodding. As he proceeded to tell me how Ben and Kelly had been hanging out, I couldn't help but create scenarios in my head. Ben and Kelly had been together for years, and he had dumped me for her once before.

My insecurity got the best of me and I made a hasty decision. I wasn't going to sit around and wait to see what played out between Ben and Kelly. I wasn't going to let him choose her over me again. All the old feelings of anger started to surface as I reran history over and over in my mind. I went into revenge mode before I even knew what Ben was really doing. I didn't go to Ben and talk to him about it but instead began confiding in others, like my mother and a close friend. *How did this happen? I must have made the wrong choice.*

I soon found myself on the phone, pouring my heart out to Stephen. Shortly thereafter I was standing at his doorstep, begging for forgiveness and professing my undying love. He opened the door and let me in without a second of hesitation, flashing his beautiful smile, his blue eyes looking right through me. I walked into his home and found my magic man once again.

The funny thing is, I focused on the flaws of the men I was dating, but really, I was the flawed one. I was seeking something that was all wrong, vacillating between relationships. I couldn't make a decision and stick to it, so I ended up hurting people before they could hurt me. It was my way of protecting myself.

I was sneaking around with Stephen, waiting for the right time to end my relationship with Ben. Then one night, in the pouring rain, I went to Stephen's place. I was soaking wet but excited to see him. There was something so romantic about this scenario, like we were in the movies. I had been there only a few minutes when I heard a loud pounding on the door. I opened it and saw Ben standing there, dripping wet. He had followed me to call me out on my betrayal. As I watched him walk back to his car in the pouring rain, I saw another marriage wash away.

After the divorce was final, my relationship with Stephen went right back to where it was before I married Ben. But the things that were wrong with our relationship the first time did not magically get fixed. I was a mess, and I needed the comfort of our dysfunctional relationship.

Despite being codependent in my relationship, I needed to find independence in my life, and I wanted to find a way to support Donnie on my own. I felt like I was starting all over again.

I met a friend for dinner and she shared with me about becoming a paralegal and told me the kind of salary it provided. She seemed so put together, and I desperately wanted that. I didn't want to wait tables or work for friends' husbands anymore. I wanted something different, something better for Donnie and me.

I went to the college she told me about and listened as they explained what it would be like to be a student there. I loved history and law, so becoming a paralegal seemed like a good fit for me.

I shared my plan with my parents and they were encouraging.

They told me they would help care for Donnie while I was in class. Now the only challenge would be to find the money to pay for the tuition. I had nothing, and I was receiving no child support from Don, just the debt he had racked up before we divorced. I didn't know how I would make this work.

The next day I went to the school and explained to them my situation. Within a few minutes the student counselor helped me file for government loans, telling me I had a good chance of getting them since I was a woman and a single parent.

Before I knew it, I was sitting in the classroom taking the entrance exam. It had been a few years since I graduated from high school and I was concerned about looking smart. Yet I felt incredibly stupid sitting there, looking around the room at the other potential students and trying to remember the difference between a pronoun and a conjunction. As hours passed, I hoped and prayed that my brain would work well enough to pass the exam so I could start paralegal school.

I got accepted, but starting school was tough. I was mentally and physically overwhelmed at all the things I needed to do on a daily basis. Here I was, a young mother in need of a better education to take care of my son, sitting alongside kids just out of high school. We weren't far apart in age, but we seemed very far apart in life. They would talk about hitting the clubs after class while I had to go straight home to be with Donnie and study after he went to sleep.

I was determined to be one of the best in my class and I needed to have good study habits. There were many long nights writing essays and studying for tests. I was exhausted and wished there was another way to get ahead. But thank God for my mom, who sat with me for hours and helped me write my papers. I so wanted to make my parents proud, to show them that I was finally getting it all together.

Meanwhile, my relationship with Stephen continued to be strained and I wanted so much more than he was willing to give. I had moved on with my education and began thinking maybe it was time to move on in my love life too. I thought by jumping from one relationship to the next I could be happy. But all that was temporary. As soon as the excitement of the relationship dissipated and things got tough, I felt the need to seek happiness somewhere else, with someone else.

I started to think about finding someone who wanted to be a family with Donnie and me. So when a girlfriend asked if she could set me up on a blind date with one of the lawyers who volunteered his time in the legal studies department of my school, I agreed.

I put on a little black dress and tried to look like a real lady. We went to a swanky restaurant, where I had one of the finest meals I'd ever had, with a man fifteen years older. He was a nice guy, with dark hair and a sweet face, but small in stature. He wore a suit, a tie, and a crisp white shirt. He was established, but not my type at all. I tried to convince myself this was a good thing.

I kept telling myself to give this a try. I thought about having a better life, with money, stability, and nice things. But something didn't feel right. I felt like I was compromising, giving up my dream of finding true love, a romance with a prince charming I was madly and passionately head over heels for, just to find stability. It was disheartening.

On the second date, I found myself lying in bed, my eyes closed, dreaming of another man while making it through the sex. I woke up the next morning feeling disgusted with myself, and sick to my stomach. What had I done? It was a mistake, and now I couldn't even look him in the face, let alone think about having a relationship with this guy. I avoided all his calls and stopped all forms of contact. Still I couldn't shake the guilt over what I had done. I had made a bad decision once again.

A few weeks later, I walked into my legal studies class and found the lawyer I had gone out with, preparing to speak to our class. I didn't know how I would escape his glares. Instead of ducking out immediately after class ended, I went up to him and tried to have a brief conversation. It was extremely awkward, but there was no escaping it. I could tell he was upset about my disappearance. I told him I'd decided to stay with my boyfriend, and I wanted to be respectful of him. It was a load of crap, but it was the best I could do.

I continued on in my relationship with Stephen, hoping somehow he would change and we would be happy again. But I was dating other guys at the same time in hopes that maybe someone might take his place. I was selfish and afraid to be alone, and my inability to make a solid decision in my love life kept me from finding any real contentment.

I graduated from school and started interning at a law firm in Scottsdale. Then I applied for a job with one of the biggest law firms in Arizona. I got the job and started working in downtown Phoenix. I felt like I was finally moving up and life was going my way. My confidence started to settle in, as I felt like I was becoming something and someone important. I wanted to be the woman who had it all, which included having the perfect man to love.

Then everything came to a screeching halt. I was sitting in Stephen's bathroom, waiting for a pregnancy test to reveal my fate. Everything I had gone through with Don, my pregnancy with Donnie, and my failed second marriage raced through my head. I was finally making changes, getting my life together, and there I was, messing it all up again.

The minutes felt like hours. Finally, there it was. The test came up positive. I was pregnant. I sat there in shock, wondering what I was going to do. I didn't want to do this again. I couldn't have a baby with a man I wasn't married to and who wasn't willing to commit.

Stephen walked into the bathroom. Without a word, I walked out and got on the phone with a family member who worked at a clinic that provided abortions. My appointment was scheduled.

It was early morning when Stephen and I arrived at the clinic. Within a few minutes the nurse came out to take me into the back room. She gave me a magic pill, and before I knew it, I woke up to the doctor telling me it was all over. I felt like Alice in Wonderland.

Since I was drowsy from the medication, Stephen drove me home. He plopped me on the couch, ordered pizza, and turned on *Seinfeld*. We never spoke of that day again.

This was the end of our relationship in so many ways, but I continued to hold on. It seemed easier to stick with what I knew.

Stephen was going to move, and I kept hoping he would ask Donnie and me to live with him. I was fishing for a commitment, the next step of our relationship, when he dropped a bomb on me. He was moving in with his best friend, Anthony. I took Stephen's decision to mean he valued his best friend more than me.

I burned with rage against Stephen, and the more he talked about looking at places with Anthony, the more I became unhinged.

They finally found a place, a trendy pad downtown, close to where I worked. After Stephen moved in with his best friend, I found myself wishing I could move on, leaving our relationship behind. Every morning, as I drove by his building on the way to work, I resented him and the decision I had made to stay with him.

As the weeks passed and the tension grew, I reached the end of my rope.

Getting ready for work one day, Stephen shared with me his plans to take a trip to Europe with Anthony, something he'd always wanted to do. He was so excited as he explained it all to me. Yet I couldn't be happy for him. He had no money to buy me a ring, he was deep in debt, yet he seemed to have the money to go to Europe with his best friend. I lost it.

I gave him an ultimatum: go to Europe and we're done. He chose Europe.

As Stephen traveled to Europe, I made my way around the Arizona club scene. I was out on the town every night, ready to party. I was being wined and dined, and loving every moment of it. Love was like a drug and I was getting high, jumping from one date to the next, looking for the relationship that would bring me my next temporary fix.

During the day, I worked at the firm, keeping my head up and trying to learn the world of law. One day, some of my coworkers invited me to happy hour. I hadn't gone out with them before, but decided to do it.

I was enjoying the company of my new friends when one of them noticed a table of young, handsome, athletic guys. She started making eyes at them, and soon one of them made his way to our table. He introduced himself and told us he and his buddies were hockey players from the local team, many of them from Canada. He mentioned that one of his friends was interested in meeting me.

I glanced over and connected right away with the dark-haired, brown-eyed, handsome athlete. He made his way over and introduced himself. He was a French-Canadian with an accent, and I felt myself melt like butter. He sat across from me and bought me a drink. I couldn't wait to hear his story. I'd always wanted to marry a hockey player. It was my second choice next to rock star.

Finding comfort in relationships, I found myself incredibly happy dating Eric. He treated me like a lady, and he was exactly what I was looking for. Yet as our new relationship was starting, my old one was returning on a plane.

Stephen called me, announcing his return. He sounded so happy, which made me angry. I decided to continue with a life that didn't include him.

After a night out with Eric, I returned home to find Stephen standing on my doorstep. He had been waiting for me and wanted to talk. I told him I had met someone else while he was vacationing in Europe and it was over between us. I had moved on.

Stephen stood there, taking in every word I said. I think he was just as dependent on the dysfunction of our relationship as I was. Realizing the need to change and move on, he hugged me and we parted ways.

Eric was kind and gentle, and I fell head over heels in love with him. We would sit and listen to Celine Dion's "Power of Love" over and over again. It was the first time in forever that I could sit, laugh, and just be myself with someone. It seemed so real, so perfect. This was the kind of man I wanted to play house with, and our relationship was moving fast.

A few weeks into dating, Eric made me a special dinner. While we were eating, he reached over and grabbed my hand. Looking deep into my eyes, he told me I should always expect to be treated like a princess. It was the first time I had heard words like that from a man's mouth, and it seemed so profound that I thought he must be wrong. I had believed that all those years, in all those relationships, I had been treated right. Men had fought over me, chased me, told me they loved me as they made love to me, apologized for misbehaving and promised they would never do it again. But this was the first time that a man said something like this to me, and matched his actions with his words.

At that moment I stopped and thought about my life. It all seemed to change. I dove into this relationship head first, with a whole different outlook. Fun date nights, family dinners with

Donnie, everything seemed perfect. This was the happiness I had been searching for, the life I wanted to live.

Then Eric received news at practice that he was being traded to another team. He needed to let them know soon whether he was willing to move. He had already made his decision. When he shared it with me, I had to make a decision—one that would change my life.

9

Redeeming Love

>⊶·∘·⊷<

"I want you to love me, I want you to trust me
enough to let me love you, and
I want you to stay here with me so we can build
a life together. That's what I want."

FRANCINE RIVERS, *REDEEMING LOVE*

*As I walked into the sanctuary, I had an overwhelming fear that
everyone would know I didn't belong there. I kept hearing in my
head a list of all the things I had done wrong in my life. But as I
sat there and listened to the pastor preach a message, I thought,*
What was this beautiful thing he kept referring to, this grace?

Eric had made the decision to play for a team in New York,
which meant he would have to move there soon. He had
given me such joy and had redeemed my outlook on love and
life. He had rescued me from a dark place and opened my eyes to
what a good relationship could be like. When he asked Donnie
and me to move with him, I wrestled with the idea. It was a huge
decision. I had fallen in love with this man and his kindness, but
still there was something missing.

Finally I made my choice. I told Eric I would be staying in

Arizona. I just couldn't make a commitment to move across the country with him, to take the chance on our still young relationship, especially when I had a son to look after. I wasn't ready to leave Arizona, my family, and my friends. I had never lived away from my parents, and I couldn't figure out how I would take care of Donnie on my own, having to start from scratch in another state. I suggested we try a long-distance relationship for a while. Eric reluctantly agreed.

Eric left and got situated in New York, and before I knew it, Stephen was back on my doorstep. Although I had it in my head that I was done with our relationship, it was just so easy being with Stephen. I knew exactly what I was getting into, and I could weave in and out of it without pressure. I would spend time with Stephen, then go home and end the night with a long phone call with Eric. I'd sit on the kitchen floor and share my day with a man a thousand miles away.

I had so many emotions running through me while I listened to Eric share about his new team and his exciting explorations of New York City. I was sad, happy, afraid, and hopeful all at the same time. It was a lot to take in. I'm not sure why, but I held on to the hope that he would return someday soon and we would be together.

Within a few weeks of Eric leaving, he called. As we began our hellos I heard excitement in his voice. He told me he had some amazing news to share with me. My heart jumped, thinking he would be returning to me. Instead he let me know he was going to France to play on a team there. This was a dream come true for him and a serious reality check for me. I was shocked, losing all hope of Eric ever returning. I dreaded telling Donnie, knowing he would be devastated as well.

As we wrapped up our phone call, I knew it was time to finally let go. If it was meant to be, then we would get back together. But with Eric in a far-off country, those chances were slim. Suddenly

I woke up to the reality that I was alone. Alone in the sense that for the first time I wasn't committed to a man in a long-term relationship. It was freeing but also terrifying.

I sat on the kitchen floor for some time, reflecting over my past and imagining what was possible for the future. I decided to try dating again but with a different outlook. Despite having experienced a good relationship with Eric, this time around I didn't want any commitments. I just wanted to go out and have fun. I had been in long-term relationships since I was fourteen years old, and I longed to know what it was like to just date. So I set my sights on men with more than just good looks and the sweet dream of love. I went after guys with money and power—a bar owner, a football player, a baseball player, a lawyer, and Stephen. It was a smorgasbord of men and good times. And whenever I started missing intimacy, I could call Stephen, knowing what to expect without getting into too much trouble.

I kept telling myself this was okay, that I wasn't hurting anyone else. I justified my behavior by believing what I was doing would help me make better choices in the future.

Dating without commitment got old for a girl who had lived her entire teen life in committed relationships, and the excitement of the chase quickly dissipated. One by one, I realized that these men had no real interest in me or my son. They were just having a good time too. And although they were dating a number of women, I could tell deep down they were looking for someone who had it together and didn't need to be taken care of, a girl they could take home to Mom. I wasn't that girl. I finally understood why my mom would tell me, "Remember, Shari, men won't buy the cow if they can get the milk for free."

I started to feel lost and depressed, wondering why I wasn't good enough to find someone to love Donnie and me. How was it that I had fallen so many times for the bad boy with no money, who was barely scraping by but would spend his last dime at the bars? None of them valued me for who I was. But then again, neither did I. We were all just broken and flawed, and at this point in my life, I was frustrated with living that damaged kind of existence.

One night, I sat and cried at my parents' house, not wanting to go back to my lonely apartment. I anguished over all the years I had lost to Don and men like Stephen. Out of all those years I had only found one man who treated Donnie and me well, but I had let him go. To make it worse, I was wasting my time dating wealthy, powerful men for fun, men who always seemed to end our relationship because they had started dating other women.

Broken and on my knees, I cried out in need of redemption. *Can no one love me?* I cried myself to sleep that night in my parents' big bed and had a wonderful dream of a beautiful Cinderella wedding. It was so bright and full of happiness as I walked down the long aisle in a gorgeous gown. But as I approached my groom, I could only see his tall stature and sandy-blond hair. I woke up thinking this was just a dream. Because of my emotional breakdown the night before, my subconscious was working to give me peace. I could only hope this dream would come true someday. I really wanted my happily-ever-after, but it seemed impossible.

I arrived at work the next morning, and as I rode the elevator up to the top floor, I made the decision to stop dating. I needed to focus on more important things, like my career and my son. No more men and no more long nights of tears. I felt my heart harden to love. I was done. I wasn't going to live like this any longer.

I started doing things differently, making new plans for my life. I was on a roll!

But three weeks later, I got a call from a friend's younger brother, someone I went to high school with. His name was Matt, and he had moved back to Arizona and was readjusting. He'd run into a mutual friend of ours and decided to try to reconnect with me. I decided this wouldn't count as dating since he was a little brother to an old friend, and nothing could possibly happen.

Matt and I decided to meet at a local hotspot downtown. I walked in first, a few minutes early. When I saw him walk through the door and head toward my table, I realized that my friend's little brother had really grown up. He wasn't little any longer. In fact, he was tall and handsome.

We ordered a drink and began catching up, talking about the last several years and why he had decided to move back to Arizona. Then I challenged him to a game of pool. Matt watched with a smile as I ran the table, and something about that moment really began our friendship. Neither one of us wanted to end the night, not because we were sweet on each other, but because we were having fun and there was no pressure. It wasn't a date. It was just two friends hanging out, laughing and talking the night away.

Afterward we walked outside to continue enjoying each other's company. Matt dropped the tailgate of his little truck and turned on Alanis Morissette, and we sat and talked for hours. Music played and the stars shined up above, raining down a peaceful backdrop. Matt shared how he went to a small, private Christian college in Santa Barbara. He had played soccer there and had a brotherhood with his teammates that he hoped would continue on throughout his life.

I found myself lost in the description of his utopia, something I had never experienced. As he continued sharing, I thought, *I'm sitting next to this good Christian boy, a perfect angel, seemingly flawless in every way. And he has no idea what kind of girl he's sitting next to.* I found it difficult to share about my life since high school, afraid he would see who I really was.

Several months passed as Matt and I continued building our friendship. I was dating a young, hip Scottsdale bar owner, but that seemed to be winding down. I had a couple of fun weekend trips to Vegas planned with my girlfriends. Matt had some trips with his friends, too, and a wedding to attend in Seattle. So we were both pretty busy. But no matter where we were, we found time to talk to each other every day.

On my last Vegas trip, I started thinking about Matt differently, flirting with the idea of dating him. As I was preparing to return home that Sunday evening, Matt and I were catching up over the phone, talking about our weekends. He mentioned that he had gone on a date the previous night with his old high school girlfriend. As he shared about the evening, dinner, and then a game, I felt something burning inside me. I was jealous.

For the rest of the day I couldn't stop thinking about that conversation, about this woman Matt had gone out with. I got on the plane reeling with jealousy, yet thinking how crazy I was since we were just friends. I exited the plane, walking and talking with my girlfriends about our fun weekend, trying to shake off these jealous feelings, as we headed for the baggage claim.

As I was riding down on the escalator, I saw Matt standing at the bottom, with a baseball cap on his head and a big smile on his face. As the escalator moved me closer and closer to Matt, our last few months together played through my head. It was just like a movie. And at that moment, I knew I wanted more. He had won my heart.

Matt drove me home that night, and I felt butterflies in my stomach. My heart wanted this so badly, but my mind kept asking, *How could this good Christian boy like me or want anything to do with me?*

He was such a good friend, I figured that was why he'd shown up to give me a ride home. That was how I justified him being there. It was a way for me to guard my heart.

I decided that I wouldn't pursue him. Instead I would let him decide whether he liked me or not. I would wait and let him make the next move.

I continued to wait patiently, hoping something would happen. But we continued just as friends.

One evening, as we were driving down the freeway together headed to a game, Matt told me about the kind of woman he wanted to marry. His description sounded nothing like me. The wife he described was a perfect woman who would have his babies. I pictured a beautiful, angelic-looking woman with the sweet smell of flowers surrounding her as she fed orphans in a third-world country. He said she would be Christian and a virgin. I was neither of those things. Realizing that Matt wasn't interested in me the way I was in him, I resigned myself to being just friends with this wonderful man.

A couple of weeks later, Matt asked me to go to Santa Barbara with him for a weekend reunion with some of his college buddies. I figured we were friends, so why not? We stopped in Claremont first to meet up with his friend Rob. I could tell Matt loved this man and was excited to introduce us. Matt kept encouraging Rob and me to get to know each other better.

When we arrived at the lush green ocean front of Santa Barbara, I was breathless at the beauty of this city. We made our way to the college house, where Matt and his buddies had lived, and every time I turned around I met someone new. It was an incredible, fun-filled weekend, and I could see why Matt loved this place and these people.

As the weekend was coming to an end, I found out Matt was trying to set Rob and me up. This was surprising and a bit frustrating. I didn't need his help to find a date.

We said our good-byes to all of his buddies and my new friends, then jumped into his truck for the nine-hour trek back to Arizona.

Matt could sense my discontentment, and for the first few hours it was tense and quiet between us. Finally he broke the silence and asked me what was wrong. Frustrated, I told him that I didn't want to date Rob, and the last thing I needed was to be dating someone who lived in another state. I had tried that and it didn't work.

Matt explained his reasons for wanting to set us up, and I started to understand where he was coming from. He had good intentions. Sadly, that just made me want to date Matt even more. He was such a good man with a heart of gold.

Everything became calm between us again as we laughed and recapped the weekend. We were getting close to home when it got quiet again. Then Matt took a deep breath, looked at me, and said, "Well, what would think of dating me?"

I just about choked on my cigarette. That was the last thing I'd expected to come out of his mouth. I heard myself say, "Yes." I didn't even need to think about it.

The rest of the car ride home, I worried if this was real. *Does he know who he's getting into a relationship with? Do I know who I'm getting into a relationship with?* Here was a new college graduate, with no money and no career, taking on a woman and her young son. When I took that elevator ride a few months back, swearing off dating, I had no idea I would end up in a relationship with a good Christian boy with nothing except for his faith. I had come a long way.

We approached my house and said our good-byes, leaving each other on a high note. I walked through the door with a new attitude, dreaming of all the possibilities this relationship could bring.

Then I heard the doorbell ring. It was Matt. He smiled. "I just wanted to know if I could give you a kiss." I closed my eyes and savored the moment as we kissed for the first time. It was sweet and fresh, just like a first kiss should be. He was a real Prince Charming.

We were on our second official date when Matt asked if I

wanted to go to church with him. I thought, *Really? You want me to go to church with you? Do you know who you're asking to go to church?*

I didn't even know if I wanted to go to church. Surely the people there would look at me and know right away that I was a bad girl with a horrible past. But Matt convinced me I would like it. And at that moment I was all about impressing this boy and spending as much time with him as I could.

We arrived at church, and as I walked into the sanctuary with Matt by my side, I couldn't help but worry whether I was dressed wrong or someone might recognize me. Did they know I was a smoker, divorced, a woman with a scarlet letter on her? But I was pleasantly surprised. No one looked at me with judging eyes. Instead, it was the complete opposite. I was welcomed with open arms and smiles by everyone.

The warmth and a peace that surrounded me in that tiny building was something I hadn't felt before. This church thing could be intoxicating.

The pastor entered, and he seemed to have a glow about him. He stood at the pulpit and delivered a message I had never heard before, one about love, forgiveness, and grace. *What is this beautiful thing he keeps referring to, this grace?* He said, "We are all important to God." As I savored the thought, tears streamed down my face, and I prayed to the Lord to forgive me.

Instantly I felt a sense of peace. I'd gone to church in order to win the love of a man, but instead I *received* a love that was so much greater. I discovered the love of a man who had come to earth as a baby and died on the cross for *me*. For someone so flawed, so imperfect. He was my Savior, and I had found Him that night, but He had already been in love with me all this time.

With tears of joy rolling down my face, I dedicated my life to Christ. I knew this was the beginning of a new journey, this time with Jesus in my heart and God by my side. My life was about to change forever.

It was wonderful spending time with Matt, getting to know each other better and sharing our dreams for our lives. But I was also exhausted as I juggled two jobs while taking care of Donnie. I worked at the law firm during the day from Thursday through Saturday, then served dinner at a high-end steak house at nights. The days were long and it was a challenge to see Matt in between everything else. But just when I thought I couldn't wait on one more table, Matt would walk through the door, find a seat, order something to eat for dinner, and sit there for hours just to be with me. I had never known such love and devotion before.

The beauty of dark times is the redemption that comes afterward. I'd had so many bad relationships that when something good finally came my way I knew how to appreciate it. Being with Matt was refreshing, and I took it in and savored each moment.

It seemed like I was finally getting a chance to live a normal life with an amazing man. Still, a part of me feared this might not work because of my past. Somewhere along the line, Matt would decide he wanted something better or someone different. I had been praying for a life where I didn't have to look over my shoulder, a life where my son could grow up without a father who was constantly in and out of trouble. Now my prayers were being answered and it was all happening for me.

Then I got a call.

I returned home late from work one night and saw a message on my answering machine. It was from Don. I had already spoken to him that morning, and he was asking to see Donnie that night. He had just returned to Arizona after a long period of living in Louisiana.

A horrible feeling passed over me. I told him we already had plans, but tomorrow night might work.

Part Four

TRUST ME

Dying to Myself

Action! Watching a movie set come to life is one of the most spectacular things to observe. As the scene goes up and the cameras turn on, it's amazing how a group of people team up to work every facet, dancing around one another, filling in every necessary piece of the puzzle. It's its own little world, and everyone plays an essential part, unbeknownst to the audience, who only gets a small glimpse of what's on the screen.

As I sat in my dressing room, waiting to be called to play my role, I took a deep breath. I looked in the mirror, fixing my hair and makeup, in awe of the team who helped transform me physically into my character. Now it was time for me to do the same from the inside. Anxious, and full of butterflies, I prayed to the Lord, asking Him to go before me in the scene, thanking Him for choosing the time and place for me to be part of this story.

Walking to the set, a peace came over me as I noticed the crew hard at work, making this film come to fruition. As the director shared his vision for the scene, revealing how he saw my character, I felt at ease, knowing I was in good hands. As he explained every detail, any fear I had left dissipated and I saw the power of the story he wanted to tell. Finally, he looked at me with a smile and said, "Trust me."

Knowing I have a divine Director to guide my path, and a

team of Christian brothers and sisters behind me, is reassuring. Hearing His vision and understanding His purpose helps me to step into my role with confidence. Everything is not always happy, and there are plenty of bumps and challenges along the way, yet He remains faithfully by my side, helping me move from one scene to the next, transforming my life into the story He wants to tell. All I have to do is trust Him.

10

Refining Fires

> "Imagine yourself as a living house. God comes
> in to rebuild that house. At first, perhaps, you can
> understand what He is doing. But presently He starts
> knocking the house about in a way that hurts
> abominably and does not seem to make any sense.
> He is building quite a different house from the one you
> thought of…. You thought you were being made into a
> decent little cottage: but He is building a palace.
> He intends to come and live in it Himself."
>
> C. S. LEWIS, *MERE CHRISTIANITY*

As I looked into the face of the magic man, professing his undying love for me, the man I had been desperately head over heels for, the one I couldn't seem to be able to pull myself away from, I felt uncertain of what to do. He told me there was a young woman on her way from another state to live with him. But all this could change with one word. All I had to say was "Yes."

Life was starting to finally come together for me. So many things were happening in my life, changes I couldn't believe were taking place. I never imagined that I would be going to church every Sunday with Matt and Donnie, but it was happening. We were moving toward becoming this family I had always dreamt of. Now I was just waiting and hoping Matt would propose.

But just as walls were being knocked down in my life, a loud knock came at my door. I opened it to find myself face-to-face with Stephen. He professed his undying love for me and asked for one last chance. He said he wanted me back and believed that he could make me happy. I was torn as I looked into the face of the magic man.

Despite things going smoothly in my relationship with Matt, I stood there listening to Stephen run down our history together. I thought, *Matt really isn't my type. I've never dated a nice guy, a church-goer, someone people might think of as a preppie.* It just didn't seem to make sense. There I was, a bad girl, a misfit who had done so many sinful things in her life. I didn't think I could truly start all over again.

I recalled the night when I asked Donnie what he thought about this new man in our lives. Up to that point I hadn't been much of a mother to my little boy, but my heart was slowly beginning to change and I wanted to put him first. I wanted more for Donnie than I had given him, and it meant a lot to me to know what he thought about Matt.

Donnie was an "old soul," a sweet boy who felt deeply. When I asked him what he thought of Matt, he looked at me with his big green eyes and a knowing look and said, "He respects you." This completely blew me away. Here was an eight-year-old child talking about respect. *What could he possibly know about it?* But that moment rang truth to my ears and I knew that what this little boy said was right.

As I looked into the face of the magic man professing his undying love for me, the man I had been desperately head over heels for, the one I couldn't seem to be able to pull myself away from, I felt uncertain of what to do. As the past brought me back into the present, I heard Stephen tell me there was a young woman on her way from another state to live with him. But all this could change with one word. All I had to say was "Yes," and he would tell her not to come. Then we would be together for good.

At that moment I felt the calming presence of my Savior, whispering His love for me. He wanted more for me and was already giving it to me. Despite the fact that Matt and I didn't seem to "fit," suddenly all I could think about was my sweet, handsome prince, the one who had entered my life and truly changed it.

I was left with an important choice. I struggled for a few brief moments, then told Stephen it was over. We had nothing else to give one another and I had fallen in love with Matt. I was happy.

Stephen took a moment to answer, then respectfully hugged me and said good-bye. My heart pounded as he got on his motorcycle and took off. After watching him go, I closed the door behind me, and closed the door on the relationship I had known for so long.

Several weeks passed, and Matt and I were still going strong. Our relationship was growing as I started to dive into church and really study the Bible. We had long talks about marriage, children, and our future dreams.

We decided to go through premarital counseling classes at church to help us figure out if we were indeed a good match. We struggled with so many issues—sex, money, and of course the most obvious: I had a child. Marrying me meant Matt would become an instant dad.

Matt always made me feel like he wanted Donnie and me. He never second-guessed being a husband or a father. He was a man who walked the walk and talked the talk. It was a beautiful thing to see, as I was finally able to truly trust in a man. There were big hurdles to get over, but we were jumping.

The beauty of second (or should I say third?) chances is

that we are given a clean slate. There is no keeping count of our wrongs, and regardless of our past, we can be "princesses."

Matt planned an evening out with me that was full of surprises. As I put on my favorite black slip dress and strappy black shoes, I felt like a princess. Matt picked me up to go see the play *Romeo and Juliet*.

Arriving at the theater, we walked down the long aisle down to the third row, right in front of the stage. That beautiful love story opened the door to my own as Matt took me to dinner, then to one of the most lavish resorts in Arizona. We were both dirt poor, and this all seemed like a fairy tale of rich proportions.

Getting out of the car, I looked around at the lush green grass and flowers that lined the walkway of this beautiful hotel. As we walked inside, I was suddenly overwhelmed by the feeling that I didn't deserve this, I shouldn't be there. But Matt grabbed my hand and headed for the outdoor patio, where little white lights lit up the trees. There were two chairs in the grass, a perfect place for us to gaze at the stars.

Sitting there with Matt, all I could think about was how blessed I was to be with this man. This was the first time I had truly been in love. I didn't even feel like the old Shari anymore. Matt looked at me with deep devotion and love as he shared how he felt about us and the future plans he saw for our lives. Then he moved to a footstool, reached into his pocket, and pulled out a little red leather box with a small gold pinstripe and latch. He opened it, revealing a beautiful ring, a single diamond set high on a delicate gold band. It took my breath away.

In that moment I felt fully renewed, amazed that I was getting this chance to start fresh with the man I loved. I said yes, hugging and kissing Matt as he slipped the ring on my finger. It was like a movie as we ran into the hotel, proclaiming that we had gotten engaged, and the crowd cheered for us. We sat down at an intimate table for two, and the waitress brought us a bottle of champagne with two glasses so we could toast each other. It was magical.

Lost in the moment, we looked deep into each other's eyes. But we were quickly awakened to reality when the bill arrived. Matt chuckled as he warned me that he might not have enough money in his checking account to pay for the champagne. It seemed he had broken open his piggy bank for this night, the one filled with coins he had been saving for something special. He didn't even have quite enough money to pay for my engagement ring. His generous sister had stepped in to help him.

Matt gave the waitress his debit card and we held our breaths as we waited for her. She returned, placed the check in front of us with a pen, and said, "Thank you. And congratulations on your engagement."

We both breathed a great sigh of relief.

Things were changing, and I was changing. As I started planning the wedding, our romance continued to bloom. We spent all our time together. I left the law firm to work for Matt's family business. We were both working hard to prepare for our future.

As we spent more time together and got to know each other intimately, it became difficult to stay pure in our relationship. I found myself falling back into my old ways, thinking that if we had sex Matt would love me and need me more. I pushed for us to be together, but Matt always remind me that he could wait.

After a year and a half of dating, we made the mistake of being alone one too many times, which led us to a place we didn't want to be. We crossed the line and gave ourselves to each other. But because of the man Matt was, he said, "No more—not until our wedding night." And he meant it.

It was a long wait until that special day, but well worth it. Just another reminder of the respect and love Matt had for me, to hold me that sacred until the day we married.

Our parents were overjoyed about our upcoming marriage, and Matt's parents wanted to give their son the wedding of his dreams. As we planned the colors, invitations, flowers, and cake, it seemed more and more like a dream come true.

The final decision to be made was where this grand ceremony would take place. To our delight, Wrigley Mansion was available. A breathtaking landmark with 360-degree views of the city, built in 1932 by the chewing gum mogul William Wrigley Jr., it was the perfect place for our wedding.

The momentous day arrived, and as I stood at the top of the stairs, looking down to where Matt stood waiting, I couldn't help but smile. I walked down in my beautiful white gown, feeling pure and content. On each side of us stood three bridesmaids and three groomsmen, along with Donnie, the flower girl, and the ring bearer. My heart pounded as I realized I was living out the dream I'd had almost two years earlier about this very day. Every emotion ran through my body as Matt grabbed my hand. Instantly I felt complete. There, surrounded by family and friends, we were ready to say "I do" to our new lives together.

I felt was as if I were experiencing spring in my life again, as new beginnings started sprouting and I could see that this time things would be different.

Money was tight, but we found a foreclosed home we could barely afford. It was a mess inside and out, but in a great part of town. It definitely had potential, and Matt and I worked around the clock to fix it up.

While I spent time remodeling our house, God was doing the same with me. I was attending church and a women's Bible study, and fully appreciating my family life. However, my mind was set on not only growing this family spiritually but physically. I desperately wanted to give Donnie a little brother or sister. I ate, breathed, and slept baby. But the more I pressed for pregnancy, the stronger and more furious my endometriosis came on. I had been diagnosed with it when I was a teenager, and the pain was starting to become unbearable. I was mentally and physically broken.

As months continued, so did the scopes and treatments for my endometriosis. I began losing hope. I couldn't understand how I could have a wonderful husband and son but no little baby to continue our family. I was beside myself in grief and worry for Matt. More than anyone I knew, he deserved to be a dad, and I couldn't give him one child.

Matt and I began discussing the possibility of adoption. It was looking like the only hope for us to have a child.

Matt and I planned a trip to Brazil for a friend's wedding. We were thrilled to be taking some time away to relax and enjoy the beautiful country. We were also hopeful to adopt a little girl who was close to our family.

After landing in Brazil, we experienced lovely people, delicious food, crystal-blue waters, and white-sand beaches. We enjoyed ten days of perfection, dancing, laughing, and spending quality time together with our friends, without a care in the world.

Returning home was bittersweet. It was back to work, and reality settled in. Within a few days, we received a phone call that the beautiful baby girl in Brazil had been born, but we hadn't been chosen to be her parents. I was devastated.

Grieving over the decision that we weren't going to be parents, I began to feel sick. As each day passed I felt worse. I started to believe I had contracted a disease while we were in Brazil. I was so worried, I headed to the doctor to figure out what was happening. He informed me that I would continue to be sick for the next few months because I was pregnant! I'd expected the doctor to tell me I was dying. Instead he told me I was going to bring new life into the world.

I was so excited, I couldn't wait to tell Matt the good news. I just needed to figure out the perfect way to do it. When he arrived home, I handed him some McDonald's french fries. As he started to eat one, he exclaimed, "What's this?" When he saw the pregnancy test I had left for him in the fries, he said, "Gross!" Then suddenly it hit him what this meant.

Matt was so happy, and we both started crying. He's never looked at McDonald's french fries the same way.

I had a wonderful pregnancy and enjoyed every minute of it. I went into labor at six months and again at just over eight months. Three and a half weeks early, our baby wanted out in the worst way. Matt and I were blessed with Levi James, a beautiful, healthy boy. He was perfect, and he stole Matt's heart from the moment he arrived.

Levi was a fighter, and he had to fight hard over the first few years of his life. Because he had been born early, he ended up with Respiratory Syncytial Virus. He had to fight that illness over and over again. Levi was also diagnosed with eczema, double hernias, and excessive drooling, and he needed to be tested for cystic fibrosis. I couldn't believe the child we had been longing for forever was facing so much illness and disease.

I was tired and worn out, but continued to hope for the best. With all the doctor visits, stress built as Matt worked hard to help the family business. Donnie trudged his way through school, while helping me as much as a big brother could.

The cystic fibrosis testing was tough, but Levi was a trooper. Waiting for the diagnosis to come back was the longest twenty-four hours of our lives. Thankfully, the results were negative.

Still, Levi continued to get sick. Every time this poor child had a new tooth break through, the pneumonia came on again. When he was on his fourth round of pneumonia, I wanted answers. I explained all the symptoms to the doctors, let them know what

I had observed that led to another round of illness. But no one listened, and the doctors discarded my theories.

Finally one young doctor believed me. He decided to get Levi's double hernias fixed and was hopeful that this was the start to get his little body healthy. At two and a half years old, both hernias were repaired. Within six months, Levi was finally starting to look and act like a healthy boy.

I was now ready for my next baby. Matt and I had been trying, but to our chagrin, nothing was happening. I had several medical issues surface all at once, which added to my endometriosis. My so-called fairy-tale life was hit with a serious dose of reality.

Matt and I went to a fertility specialist, hoping to figure out why we couldn't get pregnant again. There's nothing like visualizing your life a certain way and finding out that what you really want is impossible.

The doctor told tell me I was no longer ovulating, even though all the tests showed that I was. With our hope that God would still allow me to get pregnant, we continued to try.

As we prayed and hoped for another baby, we watched everyone around us getting pregnant and growing their families. It seemed we were getting further and further away from our dream of adding another little person to our family. I began questioning God. *How can this be happening to me and Matt? We have everything to offer a child.*

My heart broke with each denial, until finally I released my pain. Then I sat before the Lord and simply asked, "What do You want me to do? What is it that You have planned for my life?"

Before I knew it, the Lord answered my prayers.

11

Hollywood Hills

>─┤◆├─◆─┤◆├─<

"I do not know why there is this difference, but I am
sure that God keeps no one waiting unless He sees that
it is good for him to wait. When you do enter your
room, you will find that the long wait has done you
some kind of good which you would not have had oth-
erwise. But you must regard it as waiting, not as camping. You must keep on praying for light: and of course,
even in the hall, you must begin trying to obey the rules
which are common to the whole house. And above
all you must be asking which door is the true one; not
which pleases you best by its paint and paneling."

C. S. LEWIS, *MERE CHRISTIANITY*

*It was morning and there I was walking down the once bustling
Sunset Boulevard, now empty except for the people heading off
to work. As I stood there looking around at all the billboards,
trendy clubs and fancy hotels, tears started rolling down my
face. Dejected and totally discouraged, it seemed like my dreams
would never come true. My phone rang and I didn't recognize
the phone number. I answered it, hearing a pleasant voice.*

After some time had passed, I finally accepted the fact that I would not be having any more children. While I waited for God to open the next door in my life, I waited on customers at Hebrews, the coffee shop Matt and I had started at our church.

One Sunday morning, a customer entered and sat at a table. I walked over to pour him a cup of coffee. He looked at me strangely, then asked, "Have you ever thought about doing commercials?"

At first I thought this guy must be crazy, or maybe he used this as a pickup line. But as he continued to share about this commercial he was casting, I realized it was a straightforward question. He invited me to audition. I wasn't sure what I was doing, but I decided to go. I had nothing to lose. Besides, I needed to get out of the boat and see what the Lord had in store for me.

Walking into a room full of people, I didn't think I stood a chance, but I managed to land the job. I was on the way to the next season of my life, an exciting journey that would be all about timing and patience.

I pursued a career in acting, visualizing a whole new life for myself. Working with an acting coach in Arizona, I hoped that someday soon I would become a star. Commercial after commercial came, and then an audition for a low-budget sci-fi movie filming in Arizona. This was my first film audition, and although I went prepared, I was nervous to be reading with the leading man. Twenty-four hours later, I was asked to do a screen test. Then they offered me the role.

It's difficult to let go of the things we want so desperately, but sometimes God uses that obedience to move us to the next place on the journey. I felt like I was gaining a new lease on life as my resume expanded with work on independent films, commercials, and print ads.

Show business didn't come without its own set of challenges. There was a lot of rejection, and competition, as I auditioned against thousands of people for each little job. After a while it got tough to keep hearing "no." I still felt a sadness about not having any more babies, but I could see the Lord working in my life. I had a new calling, and I was excited to answer.

A true moment of listening to God made way for a giant leap in my career. I was in Los Angeles doing a pickup day for "Easy Rider: The Ride Back," sitting in a beautiful restaurant at the hotel where my family was staying. Waiting for my family to arrive, I was enjoying dinner alone when a man walked in and sat in the cozy waiting area across from me. Suddenly I heard the Lord tell me, "Go introduce yourself to this man. His name is Chaz Corzine."

At first I brushed it off, wondering if I was going crazy. *If I do something like that in a place like this, he's going to think I'm a high-priced prostitute.*

There was no way God was telling me to do this, so I continued eating my dinner. I heard the voice again, telling me the exact same thing. This time I decided to listen. I got up and walked over to the man, who was working on his phone. When he looked up, I said, "Excuse me, but are you Chaz Corzine?"

He looked slightly perplexed, like he didn't know how to answer the question. Finally he responded, "Yes, I am."

I was hit with disbelief and excitement at the same time. As I explained who I was, he looked relieved. He chuckled and said, "I was worried you were coming over here to tell me to stop taking pictures of you with my phone."

We spoke until when my family walked in. I left wondering what the purpose of our conversation was, especially since we didn't even exchange phone numbers.

The next morning I found myself on Sunset Boulevard, completely discouraged. What was I doing there? Was this really what God wanted for my life?

My phone rang. I picked it up and heard of Chaz Corzine's voice. He had managed to get my number and was only in town for one more day. He wanted to take me around to his friends in Los Angeles and see if I had "it"—what everyone in Hollywood was looking for. I was blown away and couldn't believe this was happening.

Chaz Corzine picked me up and we went to CBS Radford. As we drove onto the lot, I had this overwhelming feeling that God was speaking to me again. In and out of offices, Chaz introduced me to his friends. I realized there was so much I needed to have as an actress.

As we pulled off the lot, Chaz informed me he was going to call one of his good friends to help me find an acting coach. Moments later, his phone rang, and on the phone was Jim Caviezel. I was amazed. Jim Caviezel recommended that I see a man named John Kirby. He would know what I needed and whether or not I had what it took to be an actress.

Before the day was over, I had received invaluable information as well as meetings with Hollywood executives and others to help me start my career. I couldn't believe this was happening. I began crying, but rather than the tears of frustration from my past, this time they were tears of joy. Life was good and I could see everything coming together.

I worked constantly on commercials, print ads, and bigger-budget films, feeling like I was living a dream and life could only get better.

Despite my excitement, no one in my family, including my husband, was as hopeful about my "calling" as I was. We had many fights, because no one could understand why I'd want to leave Arizona to start over as an actress in California. It was a long shot, a one-in-a-million chance of my becoming a star. I often heard from my closest friends, "You're too old to be an actress."

Many nights I cried myself to sleep, asking the Lord to direct my path and to open my husband's heart to be in line with mine.

We sold our home, and Matt gave me a choice: use the money to move to California or to buy our dream house and live in Phoenix among the people we loved. Influenced by the fact that everyone thought I was a dreamer for wanting to be an actress, and not feeling like I could leave everyone, I chose the house.

Every time we picked a lot in the neighborhood, something fell through and it didn't happen. It took three lots before we finally started building. Ironically, the lot we ended up with was right next to Stephen and his family. Quite a bit of time had passed, and we were all friends, so it worked out.

The day we moved in was bittersweet. It was a hot day in July and no one showed up to help us except my mom and dad. I felt like I had made the wrong decision. We managed to get it all done, but as I looked around the huge, beautiful house, it felt empty.

Life should have been perfect. The house was gorgeous and in a neighborhood full of our family and friends. We called it "The Compound." I had everything a girl could want, but I was dying inside.

Matt was focused on helping out the family business, and though I totally respected him for providing for our family, I was frustrated with our situation. By the time he came home at night, he was completely exhausted and emotionally spent. He and his father were very different people and they ran things in different ways, which caused friction at work. Many days started and ended with fights between the two of them. This put pressure on our relationship as well.

The holidays came and went, and I could barely stomach bringing in 2008. With every year that rolled around, I hoped that would be "my year," that things would finally happen for me as an actress. Yet every new year was the same. However, within a few days of toasting to 2008, my phone rang and it was Karen Ray, the casting director from *The Young and the Restless.*

Despite my doubts and frustrations with God over how my life was going, He seemed to remain faithful. He had a plan and He knew how it was going to go. It didn't always seem to line up with the way I thought it was supposed to be. But He continued to surprise me. And just as things seemed hopeless, He would show me that He had been by my side all along, leading the way, guiding my life exactly the way He knew it should go. He was just sliding in one piece of the puzzle at a time.

Karen Ray asked if I would audition for the role of Carole, a sassy, upscale Realtor. I immediately agreed, ecstatic. Matt and I jumped in the car and headed west. But two hours into the drive, our car broke down. I could see Matt's frustration and stress over how much it would cost to fix the car.

Even with our detour, we still made it to California with a little time to spare. I walked into CBS excited. I couldn't believe I was there, with posters of stars everywhere. I walked down the hallway captivated, hopeful that one day my picture would be up there too.

Within an hour, Karen Ray had finished my audition and I had a role on *The Young and the Restless.* I think my family heard me screaming all the way in Arizona!

Matt and I celebrated that night, but then he had to return to Arizona, leaving me to work the following day filming at CBS. I couldn't believe this was happening as I walked onto the studio to get my hair and makeup done. I felt like a princess, and this was just the beginning.

The show seemed to run smoothly, and it felt natural as I stood on my mark waiting to shoot my scene. However, as I stood face-to-face with these stars I had watched for years, it was hard for me to contain my joy.

I wrapped the day and returned to my hotel room to see a message on my phone. It was Jon Erwin, a director who was shooting a music video. He asked me to call him back. Another wonderful contact thanks to Chaz.

When I called Jon, he asked me if I knew of the group Casting Crowns. I told him, "Of course I do. In fact, they're one of my favorite bands." He told me he was filming the video for their song "Slow Fade," which was going to be the theme song for the new movie *Fireproof.* He said that he and his brother, Andy, wanted to hire me as the lead actress in the video.

I pinched myself. I had a soap role *and* I was going to be flying to Alabama to star in a Christian music video!

Landing in Alabama, I was overwhelmed by the kindness I was shown. Although it was already nighttime, I stopped by the location where they were filming. "Slow Fade" was a song about choices, and how one small decision can change the course of our lives. *If you had the chance to make the same choice, would you do it again?* I too had recently made a big choice in my life.

Despite doing well professionally, I was going through my own personal mess. My endometriosis was getting worse, and after filming I'd have to return home to have a surgery that meant I would no longer be able to have babies. I did my best to put that out of my mind for the next several days as I filmed "Slow Fade." It was an intense shoot, and I played a wife dealing with the compromising decisions made by her family. But through the story this video was telling, God worked out a lot of things in my own life, letting me witness what "bad choices" might look like and how damaging they could be to a family. Despite all that angst, I enjoyed every moment of filming and was thrilled to be in a music video that would be part of such an important film.

I flew home with tons of stories to share with Matt, knowing the next day we would face our own big family decision. Despite this being a life-changing choice for our family, I went into the hospital with a complete sense of peace, knowing Matt was there by my side.

Surgery went longer than expected since the endometriosis was worse than they thought it would be. I had to stay in the hospital for a few more days of recovery. But we both continued to be assured that everything would be fine.

When Friday morning arrived, the day I was to leave the hospital, the nurse came to remove my catheter. Unfortunately, my body was still anesthetized and unable to get rid of fluids. The pain worsened as fluid and pressure built up inside me without a way to come out. On Saturday I was given heavy drugs to help ease the pain, but nothing helped. The doctors ran a few tests, and within an hour they found the blockage. It was all right there on the X-rays, yet no one did anything.

Sunday rolled around, and I was still in awful pain. With no doctor around, my body seemed beyond repair. I gained thirty pounds of fluid in forty-eight hours. I was shutting down—renal failure, heavy drugs, and fluid building around my back and bones. The nurses and the on-duty physician told Matt to start calling my family.

Monday morning arrived, and finally so did the hospital's chief of staff, who happened to be a urologist. He took one look at me and said, "Clear my schedule now. We have to get her into surgery or we're going to lose her." People started moving quickly, and the next thing I knew I was waking up from a deep sleep. I heard the doctor say, "You're a miracle…or at least your bladder is."

I had survived, but it would take eight months of recovery, four more surgeries, months of stints in my ureters, and lots of bed rest. There was no more *Young and the Restless,* or any other acting jobs for that matter.

The road to recovery was full of anger and grace. It seemed I was on my way to stardom, only to have it taken away from me.

How could God open a door only to have it slam shut in my face? He had saved my life for a reason. But what was that reason? I thought I finally had Him figured out only to realize I had no idea what He was up to. I thought I had begun to rediscover the Lord and His grace for me. I was so overwhelmed by this dark time in my life. Empty and confused, I cried out to God for answers. But all the Lord would say to me was "My grace is sufficient."

With plenty of down time, I began to reflect on my life and how I had behaved with friends and family, and most of all what kind of wife and mother I had been. I prayed about where the Lord was leading me, what His purpose was for my life. It was time to be bold, to step out in faith.

I continued to search for answers from God, but for eight months He kept telling me the same thing: "My grace is sufficient." It was quite frustrating. There were lots of ups and downs, good days and bad ones, but it seemed like the bad came more often than the good.

One Sunday evening in November, Matt asked me to go to church. I didn't really want to go, but I did. The pastor began his sermon with 2 Corinthians 12:9, "He has said to me, 'My grace is sufficient for you, for my power is made perfect in weakness.' Most gladly, therefore, I will rather boast about my weaknesses, so that the power of Christ may dwell in me." I knew the Lord was speaking directly to me.

For the next couple of months I prayed over every detail of my life. I prayed over my marriage, the new business Matt and I had started, our house, my career, my family, Donnie at college in California, and Levi hating school. I finally came to a breaking point. But rather than fight God, I decided to give up every expectation I had placed on Him and on my life. I prayed, *I'm willing to get out of the boat and do whatever You want me to do.* As I prayed, the Lord took me to my Bible and showed me Acts 20:24: "I do not consider my life of any account as dear to myself, so that I may finish my course and the ministry which I received from the Lord Jesus, to testify solemnly of the gospel of the grace of God."

It was all starting to come together. The Lord was growing me and preparing me to work for His kingdom. I was finally starting to understand that His grace was all I needed. I had to stop being a "people pleaser" and instead be a "God pleaser."

Something major happens when you are faced with losing your life. You start to become more decisive, leaning toward "just do it" rather than "maybe I shouldn't." Realizing my life had been saved for a purpose pushed me to get out of the boat and into the water.

Matt and I had just faced a couple of the roughest years of our lives together, and it was time for a change. The Lord put it on my heart that it was time to leave Arizona and make the move to California. I went to Matt and explained how God had placed this on my heart and how He had torn down every idol in our lives so that He and His will could be first.

Hesitant, Matt agreed, but with several conditions. He listed all the things that needed to happen before we could move to Los Angeles.

God has a way of working things out, especially when you challenge Him with your needs. Lo and behold, He gave us exactly what we needed financially, down to the penny, for three months of rent in Los Angeles.

Matt wanted to find a place that would rent to us month-to-month, in the area we wanted to live so that Levi could go to a particular school. That happened as well. We ended up with the most amazing apartment, less than a mile from the school we wanted Levi to attend.

The Lord was pushing every door wide open for us. Now it was our turn to move.

12

October Baby

"To be human is to be beautifully flawed."

Officer Mitchell, *October Baby*

God had given me a new purpose. Everything that I thought I knew and expected from Him was not nearly what He expected from me. God wanted so much more for my life. I just had to stop and listen. His path was so much greater, so much more impactful than I could've ever imagined. God had great plans to use this flawed woman.

Arriving in Los Angeles, I immediately felt like I was home. We'd just started moving into our new apartment, unpacking boxes, and settling in when I received a call from Donnie. He sounded a little on edge. He told me Don was being released from prison in a couple of days.

I took a deep breath, full of anxiety, contemplating what this meant for Donnie and me, realizing the impact this would have on our lives.

He said Don would be allowed to live in either Phoenix or Texas, because of his parole. And he had chosen Texas so he could be with his family.

I immediately started praying for protection and peace for me and my family. I felt somewhat unhinged knowing he was out, but I knew it would happen eventually and that I just needed to trust God.

A little over four months after we moved to Los Angeles, things weren't going exactly as I had hoped. My dream of acting was turning into a nightmare, and I was on the verge of quitting. I had been studying with my acting coach, John Kirby, and was in a class with actors who had college theatrical studies backgrounds and had been working in Hollywood for some time. I, on the other hand, had no idea what I was doing. Despite having had a handful of acting jobs, I felt like I was starting all over again.

I spent each night memorizing dialogue, preparing characters, and rehearsing scenes for my class. Twenty minutes on stage seemed overwhelming, and my acting coach was stretching me, teaching me how to work in a space with other actors, how to bring a character to life. He wanted me to be the best I could be, and I was working hard to get it right, but I seemed to miss every beat. Confused and frustrated, I felt like I had misunderstood God again. Had my own aspirations gotten in the way of what He wanted?

I stood in the shower on a wintery morning, crying my eyes out. I had convinced my family to move to Los Angeles for a silly dream that would never come true. I didn't have an agent, I couldn't get an audition, and I had lost all confidence when it came to acting class. Defeated and desperate, I prayed for God to just tell me what He wanted me to do. I thought I had figured out God's purpose for my life, but maybe His plans were to take me somewhere completely different. I felt like such a failure.

I stepped out of the shower and wrapped myself in a towel. I looked at my phone and saw I had a message. A casting director had called me, someone I had auditioned for in the past. She wanted to take me to an audition for a one-liner in a new movie she was casting. She asked if I would also prepare for a larger role, the mom, which was a lead. She told me it was a long shot, "but you never know."

God was offering me some hope, proving once again that He was right there and knew exactly where I was going. I just needed to let go and trust Him. I was excited and couldn't wait to call Matt to tell him the good news.

Right before the holidays I went in for my audition. Two casting directors and the director were there. I had prepared the best I could and I gave it my all. When I was done, the director looked up, shook his head, and said, "Great."

I looked at the casting director and the reader and saw tears in their eyes. I figured I must have done well...or they both had bad allergies.

The audition gave me some hope. I held on to the belief that things were about to change. Even if I didn't get the part, I figured I could chalk it up to exercising my craft and continue focusing on my life in Los Angeles.

I spent a lot of time checking my phone, hoping to get a call telling me I had gotten the role in the film. Then I got a message from a California phone number I didn't recognize. But it wasn't the call I was hoping for. Instead it was Don's sister, Donna. In a shaky voice she told me Don had been killed in a car accident a few days earlier. He had been driving down a dirt road in Texas, late at night, with his girlfriend. When he turned a corner, the car ran off the road and hit tree. They were both killed instantly. The family was trying to get ahold of Donnie to let him know the news about his father and about the funeral.

I was in a state of shock, with so many emotions swirling around inside of me. Mostly I was brokenhearted for Donnie, who'd never had the chance to talk with Don face-to-face after his release from prison. I felt awful that Donnie would never have real closure with his biological father.

A few weeks had passed since my audition when I finally received the news that I had landed the lead role as the mother in *Not Today*. I would be playing opposite John Schneider. Bo Duke! I'd been crazy about him as a young girl, and I couldn't believe this was happening to me. Apparently God had plans for me, and it wasn't to quit acting after all.

Life is all about timing: God's timing and not my own. God was still cleaning up things from my past, moving through other people's lives, and clearing the clutter from my path so I could walk down it confident and with the right frame of mind as He prepared me to be in front of the camera.

The holidays came and went, and as spring approached, problems with the movie production and permits kept coming up. It was looking like *Not Today* was going to become *not ever*.

I was driving home on the 101 freeway with Donnie, sharing with him about my career frustrations, when my cell phone rang. I looked down and saw that Jon Erwin was calling.

Jon and I had worked together on the Casting Crowns music video "Slow Fade," and I was curious what he wanted. I picked up the phone, and Jon and I started in right where we had left off the last time we spoke. He informed me that he and Andy were shooting their first feature film, *October Baby*, and they had a part in it for me. He didn't want to elaborate. Instead, Jon wanted me to read the script and see if I liked the character. He was excited to hear my thoughts.

I couldn't stop thinking about the doors that were flying open.

When I arrived home, the script was there waiting for me. Matt had printed it out and was just as excited as I was. We stared at the script cover, with Rachel Hendrix on the front, and Matt said, "Wow, she really looks like you."

I walked into the family room, sat on the couch by the fireplace, and started to read. The script began with a young woman, Hannah, preparing to hit the stage when she finds out that she's adopted…and then discovers why she was adopted. Tears rolled down my face as I realized this young woman had survived an abortion. I kept reading with great anticipation, wondering what would happen next…and when I would see my character.

As I approached page eighty-five, I began to think the Erwins had forgotten to put my character into the script. I turned the next page and saw an incredible dialogue between Hannah, who was still searching for her birth mother, and the nurse who had signed off on her birth certificate. I hung on every word as the nurse told Hannah about her birth mother, Cindy Hastings, a successful lawyer who had tried to abort her child. I imagined the conversation, completely wrapped up in the moment. Suddenly I realized, *The nurse is talking about me. Not my character, but me, Shari.*

I turned the next page and saw a picture so overwhelming I knew right then I was supposed to say yes to this role. The picture was taken at the same church where I had filmed the music video "Slow Fade" two years prior. After the shoot I'd returned home to have a much-needed surgery, one that nearly took my life. It was as if God was reminding me that I'd been given a second chance and He was working out all the details of my journey.

I continued to flip through the script. When I got to the dialogue between Cindy Hastings and her husband, and she tells him what she has done and the shame that she feels, I went back in time to a moment that was private and heartbreaking for Matt and me.

We had been married for six years and I was admitting to him everything, including details about old boyfriends and past sins, and finally about the abortion I'd had long ago. It was a hard topic to discuss since Matt and I had been desperately trying to have another child after Levi. Telling him I had taken the life of a baby when I couldn't give him one was a heartbreaking but grace-filled moment. Matt had extended his arms of love to me, just as the husband did to Cindy Hastings in the movie script. I had my confirmation.

With tears running down my face and a very heavy heart, I knew I needed to call Jon Erwin right away. I walked into the kitchen, where Matt was cooking dinner. Before he could even ask me about the script, I blurted out, "It's about an abortion survivor and my character is the birth mother."

His face fell. He understood the pain I was feeling because of my own experience. He spoke to me about two children who had gone to school with Donnie, both abortion survivors who had been severely injured during the procedure.

I called Jon Erwin and shared my story with him. When I finished, my face soaked with tears, there was silence. Then Jon said, "Wow, wow, wow."

In that moment something opened up the gates to a new beginning. I was relieved to be finally sharing a hidden shame of my past.

When he told me the part was mine, excitement boiled up inside of me. I immediately booked a private coaching session with John Kirby. I knew it would be a challenge to take the audience on a journey beginning in one place and ending in another. And I had about five minutes of scene time to make it happen.

John and I worked on the scene, and we discussed the character, her frantic type-A nature, and how she would operate in the space of the scene. Leaving John's Hollywood studio, I felt a little disappointed. I was finally working on a movie, but I only had one scene of dialogue. Self-doubt consumed me and my excitement turned into anxiety. I was booked to star in two films, one that seemed would never shoot and another I was only in for five minutes.

Discouraged, I felt like maybe I had pushed doors open that should've remained locked.

I took my script and headed to the bathtub. I rested there for a few minutes and prayed about the hurt I felt, discontent flowing through my blood. I couldn't come to grips with the idea of just five minutes on the screen. I kept thinking, *I barely get to show what I can do. I want more time. I want to show people my acting skills. I want them to like me as an actress. I want to tell the writers the birth mother is more important than five minutes of screen time!* All these frustrations raced through my head until I was in tears.

My deepest desires were getting in the way, and my need to feel important was clouding the reality of what God was doing. All I could think about was me.

I picked up the script and read my part again, thinking about the scene, examining every word and walking through the movements in my head. Then I got on my knees in the bathtub and burst into tears, telling God, *This isn't enough. I want more!*

Within second of my doing this, God stepped in. He told me to confess my sin of abortion. I dropped the script by the side of the bathtub and curled up tight into a ball. I cried out for forgiveness. I asked the Lord to forgive me for what I had done. I kept repeating, "I'm sorry. I'm so sorry."

Then the Lord revealed something to me. He showed me the most beautiful little girl standing in heaven. She looked at me with a sweet face. Behind her were many children running and playing in the light. They looked so happy.

Then God showed me a sea of women's faces peeking out through the darkness. They were shoulder to shoulder, pressed tightly together, and there were so many of them. As I looked into each face God said to me, "This is for them."

I didn't know what that meant. I wanted to go back and stand in front of the little girl.

When it was all over, I sat back down in the bathtub and gathered my thoughts. God has a way of taking us out of the equation and putting Himself into it. Suddenly a perfect kind of peace took over my body and thoughts, as if God had given me my own personal baptism.

I was being narrow-minded, but God reminded me that He is huge. Living in the moment, our lives might look like one thing when really it's something so much bigger than we can understand.

I was concerned about how big my role was in this film, when God was doing something much greater. He was going to impact other people, and He was starting with me. Humbled and amazed, I knew He was moving. I just needed to have faith.

I reached over the side of the tub and grabbed the script, holding it tightly. I had a newfound appreciation for the story I was about to be a part of.

Within a few days, I received an e-mail followed by a call telling me that the producers of *Not Today* were putting together the shooting schedule. Shortly after that, I received notice about the schedule for *October Baby*. They were shooting back to back. I would shoot *Not Today* first in Orange County, have one day home in Los Angeles, then fly to Birmingham, Alabama to film *October Baby*. I noticed John Schneider's name on both e-mails and realized we would be working together on both films.

I headed to Orange County to have dinner with producers, directors, and fellow actors of *Not Today*. I had heard what a powerhouse John Schneider was, that he was wonderful to work with but that I needed to make sure to stand my ground with him. They were right. From the moment I met John, he was charismatic, dynamic, magnetic. I had great respect for him. But he was a serious pro, and I quickly let go of any doubts I had about being in a scene with him. I was motivated to take on the role of his wife.

With cameras rolling, I lay in bed, having a breakdown over my son who was in India, desperately trying to help another man find his daughter. John Schneider held me like a loving husband and shared a John Wayne story with me. It was a sweet moment and I witnessed what a talent John was. What fortune I had to be able to work with him as my leading man.

When we wrapped *Not Today*, John and I told each other, "See you in Birmingham." It had been great getting to know John, sharing about our families and talking about our upcoming film with Jon and Andy Erwin. I was excited to be going to Alabama. Even if it was just for a few days to film a short couple of scenes, I felt like a movie star.

After arriving there, I got to my hotel and met with the wardrobe stylist, Anna, who came with her brand-new baby girl. Her assistant arrived at my door with incredible clothes for me to try on. Anna helped me in and out of outfits, snapping my picture while sharing about her work and family. I felt like I had known her my whole life.

Cecil Stokes picked me up in the early morning for my first day of shooting and we became fast friends. As I climbed into the large van, I met Rachel Hendrix, the beautiful young woman who would be playing my birth daughter. Cecil thought it would be good for us to meet prior to shooting our scene together. After grabbing Starbucks, we talked a little bit about our backgrounds as we drove to the set.

We pulled up to a large business building, and my heart started racing with excitement. I was looking forward to seeing my friends Jon and Andy.

Inside, tons of people were hustling, preparing for the big day of shooting. The Erwins approached me and greeted me warmly. Then I was shuffled over to the set where we would be shooting the first several scenes. It was so surreal.

After walk-throughs of each scene, I was taken into wardrobe and makeup so Anna and the Erwins could make final decisions about clothes and hair. In the makeup chair I got ready for my transformation.

Rachel entered, and we went through our lines for the first big scene. My hair was pulled into a bun, and I slipped on the gray dress and my own black heels, which gave me comfort and confidence. I grabbed my script, prop briefcase, and purse and walked out of there as Cindy Hastings.

I walked onto the set: an office with a large desk, pictures of my little girl, and child's artwork. It reminded me so much of the office I'd worked in years earlier as a paralegal. It felt familiar, as if I'd just walked into my past. I said a short, silent prayer as the crew finished setting up lights, camera, and sound.

Action! I walked into my office and saw Rachel as Hannah, looking at my things, her back to me. As I packed things into my briefcase, I mentioned I was in a hurry to meet my husband and daughter. Hannah turned to look at me, a lost look on her face, as she delivered a blow. "I was born on…"

At that moment, I looked at Hannah and saw the little girl I'd seen in the bathtub, but all grown up. My heart raced as I looked at her, feeling shame and hurt. A pain ran through my body, and I felt like I wanted to run away. I choked up so much, I could barely remember my lines. Many emotions rushed through my mind.

In character, I went into survival mode. I picked up the phone to cancel my lunch, not wanting to get caught.

Then my on-screen husband entered the scene. He asked who this young girl in my office was. All I could see was Matt's face. I felt shame, looking at my husband and thinking what a godly man he was for marrying someone like me.

Cut! I was relieved when the scene was over. I went directly to wardrobe to prepare for my next scene. As my clothing was changed and my hair was reworked, so were my emotions.

I sat in the makeup chair and read through the scene. There was no dialogue, just me walking into my office and seeing a note from Hannah. There was no way to prepare myself for that, so I just prayed that the emotions and movements would come naturally.

Andy, the director, shared a few thoughts and I said a little prayer. Then—action. I walked into the office and looked at the note on the desk, along with a hospital bracelet. Many thoughts ran through my mind, but what stood out was the decision I had made all those years ago, the decision to have an abortion.

I picked up the note and the bracelet, walked to the door, closed it, and leaned against it. The fresh scent of the note overtook me, bringing on an incredible wave of brokenness and shame, flooding my body until I couldn't control it any longer. I slid down and sat on the floor as real emotions completely overwhelmed me. Tears ran down my face. I was so broken and as I sat there, staring at the note, I started heaving.

Suddenly I was no longer on the set. It was just me and God. I heard His voice telling me, "It is done. You have been forgiven." There was a strong sensation of peace and love, like I was sitting on God's lap as He held me tightly.

Cut. The set fell silent, and I heard myself crying. Snot was everywhere. I had forgotten all about the crew and other people surrounding me.

Anna came over to sit with me, wrapping me in a hug. I looked at her tear-streaked face. Andy told everyone to give us a moment alone. Anna and I remained, crying together. She was celebrating her new baby girl while I was mourning the loss of mine.

After a few moments, Anna wiped my face and walked with me to the makeup room. I was going to need a complete rework for any additional takes. After a second take, the scene was done.

I was emotionally drained, not having much more in me, but there was still one more scene that would shoot that evening, one that I thought would complete my journey.

Action. I stood with the actor playing my husband, the note in my hand. Grasping it tightly, I explained to him who the young woman in my office was and telling him about the abortion. I felt as if I were reliving a piece of my history, remembering the moment I had to tell my real husband, Matt, everything.

As I finished, I looked up and saw the look on my screen husband's face. He looked truly broken. But then his expression changed to one of love and compassion. Without saying a word, he opened his arms and embraced me, giving me love just like Matt had done so many years earlier.

I left Alabama the next day with a feeling of being complete. I had been healed and forgiven. God had taken my flaws and my shame, and He used them in the most unbelievable way while allowing me to release it all to Him.

I returned home and shared with Matt everything that had happened. He reassured me the Lord was going to use this experience. He was going to use me.

A year passed, and in the fall of 2011, I received a call from Andy Erwin, who was at a film festival in California where they would be screening *October Baby*. He asked me if I would be willing to share my experience of what happened on the movie set and why the film was so important to me. I agreed to share my story.

Andy arrived at my home with a camera man to film my testimony. My dear friend Susie was there, encouraging me and praying for me the entire time. The interview raised a lot of emotions, but this time I was filled with feelings of thankfulness and peace. I could tell the cameraman was moved, and I knew the Lord was working.

Shortly after sharing my testimony, *October Baby* screened in Mississippi. They put my interview at the end of the film.

In the middle of January, I was booked to travel, doing press for *October Baby*. Everywhere I went, I had the opportunity to share my story of forgiveness. It was amazing to see God working, to see people's lives changing, watching men and women with tears rolling down their faces as they watched the movie and witnessed my testimony at the end.

God had given me a new purpose. Everything that I thought I knew and expected from Him was not nearly what He expected from me. God wanted so much more for my life. I just had to stop and listen. His path was so much greater, so much more impactful than I could've ever imagined. God had great plans to use this flawed woman.

Before the second month of press, I signed on with the Ambassadors Speakers Bureau, and there was talk about a book deal. Things were moving fast. I prayed for my next television/film audition, then checked my e-mail and saw another speaking request. God was at work, and He sure had a plan.

I was booked at more than sixty speaking events, including "Rock the River" for Franklin Graham and hosting the "100 Million Christmas Shoeboxes" celebration for Samaritan's Purse. The Lord was giving me opportunities to share my story and my love for His people.

I was on the road for two years, speaking to thousands at maternity homes and pregnancy centers. There were so many broken people who needed healing from their experiences of abortion, adoption, and infertility. Those women in my vision didn't even begin to represent all the people God wanted to reach through me. He wanted more. And this was only the beginning.

And they overcame him because of the blood of the Lamb and because of the word of their testimony, and they did not love their life even when faced with death.

—*Revelation 12:11*

13

The Sea of Faces

＞‐◈‐◦‐◈‐＜

But the LORD said to me,
"Do not say, 'I am a youth,'
because everywhere I send you, you shall go,
and all that I command you, you shall speak.
Do not be afraid of them,
for I am with you to deliver you," declares the LORD.
Then the LORD stretched out His hand and
touched my mouth, and the LORD said to me,
"Behold, I have put My words in your mouth."

JEREMIAH 1:7–9

I had been running from my past for quite some time. I had changed my life. I was married to a good Christian man, no longer identified as the woman I had been before. My flaws had been concealed, and what people saw was the person I wanted them to see, the woman who had it all together.

But here's the thing. My flaws made me into the person I am today. They are what brought me to the sweet aroma of a Savior who loves me, who died for me and intends to use me, with all my flaws, for His glory. This is how we know how much He loves us, that despite all our imperfections, He sees us as beautiful.

I have been on an incredible journey for the last couple of

years, sharing my testimony and the grace of our Savior to men, women, and teens all over the US. God has called me to love on the broken by encouraging them to embrace their flaws and pick up their armor for His kingdom, to share with others what He has done in their lives. The power of a testimony is the acceptance of our past flaws and the ability to use them to show others that they too are loved. "And they overcame him because of the blood of the Lamb and because of the word of their testimony, and they did not love their life even when faced with death" (Revelation 12:11).

Below are just a few of the hundreds of testimonies that have been shared with me since the premiere of *October Baby*. I hope you are able to hear the voices of men and women who are beautifully flawed as they share pieces of their journey. These stories are raw and just the way they were sent to me, except in a few cases to protect privacy.

April 2014

Your testimony during DNow [a weekend event at a church in North Carolina] was very encouraging to me as a single mom… who has made some mistakes myself in life…some not so great choices. [I] walked away from God a time or two … and come back. … It was good to hear you say, "He was there all along." I know after my mom's death a year ago, it made me realize I needed Him more than ever. Thank you for reminding me that there is a godly man out there for me…and that my daughter and I are important in God's eyes. You are an amazing woman doing a great job showing God's love!!!

April 2012

A beautiful woman shared her forty-three-year journey of living with the physical and mental pain of surviving a late-term abortion. She was a young girl of just twelve years old when she was a victim of incest. The day before her thirteenth birthday, her parents whisked her off to Texas to abort the six-month baby boy she was carrying. Because of the late term of her pregnancy and the botched surgery, she almost bled to death on the operating table. She did not wake to birthday presents or a cake adorned with candles but clinging to life and the loss of a baby boy. She shared in her letter:

I cried through a lot of the movie, and really cried during Shari's performance at the end. I literally felt her pain. I stretched out my hand toward the screen, toward her. It was as though I could touch her. I whispered to God, "Please heal me and give me peace." I truly believe it was at that moment God healed me. Because of the movie I was finally able to forgive myself and was set free from the curse with which I had struggled so many years. I have total peace, and found forgiveness because of *October Baby*. I was able to let go and accept the healing.

Spring 2014

October Baby has made a huge impact on my life, as did your story. I was a failed abortion child. I was adopted at three months old by a nice Christian family who led me to Christ and saved my life. I've known my real mother my whole life, and every time I used to see her or talk to her she would bring me down and tell me God isn't real, that I don't belong in this world. After a while it affected me so much that we stopped having visits.

When I saw your movie, I watched it seven times, bawling my eyes out. Because I finally came to terms with that, I can forgive my mother, whether she accepts me or not. I told my mother I forgive her and she never spoke to me again, and it's been two years. But I'm okay. I'm free. I can live my life without thinking that I'm a mistake. I'm a child of God. So thank you. I know I've never met you, but ever since I saw your movie I felt a connection with you and I do love you. God bless. You're an amazing actress.

Spring 2014

October Baby did amazing things for my life. It made me remember that I was dead once. It made me remember that the first twenty-three years of my life were spent searching for meaning and purpose. It made me recall the nights spent weeping over my choices, staring my emptiness face-to-face, confronting my desire to be better but my lack of willingness to change. By living through the darkness of sin, I saw the worst of what I could be. I felt like nothing, like garbage. But experiencing Hannah's story, I rekindled the fire in my heart that led to my conversion. …I am a beloved child of God. I have a purpose. This has helped me immensely in my vocation as a husband and father of seven. Thanks for all you do!

April 2014

Hello, beautiful Shari!

I have wanted to message you for a while but never got around to it till now.

First, thank you so very much for liking my page. That means the world to me!

Second, I just wanted to affirm you and the lovely woman you are. Ever since I saw that interview with you from *October Baby* I was touched and moved, and immediately knew I loved you, and thought you were such a precious lady.

I just wanted to let you know that you are very loved, and I admire you very much. You are a brave and beautiful woman, Shari.

Much love your way.

November 2013

Hi. This is a bit odd for me, but I just finished watching *October Baby*. I was in tears when the birth mother part came. I have no idea why, but I felt like I needed to try to contact Shari, as crazy as I'm sure that sounds. I am surprised I found this site… although it makes me quite nervous. I've never really tried to contact an actress before, because of course, they're famous and I'm not. But I felt led to this, so here goes.

I am a birth mother. I just placed my son on October 4th of this year, the day after my 28th birthday. I could no longer care for him. I raised him for the first 4 1/2 months of his life, so giving him up just crushed me. This is the first time I have ever seen a movie that I felt like I was meant to see. Felt like someone understood what I feel. I cannot even explain it. I could write pages right now, but it's late so I'm going to keep it short and sweet. I know it's a lot to ask…but if you could just pass this note on to Shari, I would be so grateful. God bless, and thank you so much, Shari, for being a part of that movie. It's touched me deeply.

March 2012

Shari, your role in *October Baby* touched my soul in an incredible way. The movie just happened to be released the same week I gave my testimony about my abortion experience in front of 80 women at my church. It was one of the hardest things I have ever done in my life. Hearing your testimony at the end of the movie was like balm to my soul. Your story is so similar to mine. I also chose abortion in an effort to avoid being seen as a "failure" and tried to keep it a secret for so long. Hearing you speak those words gave me comfort in knowing that I am not alone. Like you, I also had my moment of healing with the Lord and I tear up every time I think about it. When I heard you speak about your moment all those feeling came rushing back to me and I knew exactly how you felt. God is an amazing healer and I am so grateful that you shared your story as a testimony of His healing for the world to see. I have reached out to you over the past few years since the movie has been released and each time you have responded with love and grace. I am so grateful for you and your testimony. You are a blessing to so many. Keeping doing God's work! Thank you.

Fall 2012

I was living in Colorado at the time, and my daughter and I were invited to attend the movie *October Baby* with a group of teens and my pastor's wife, the CEO of a pregnancy resource center. I had not heard of the movie and did not have much involvement with the center during that time. It was Sunday, April 15, 2012, when I saw the movie. I watched the movie and it seemed as though I never took a breath with tears streaming down my face. I knew at that moment I wanted to do something, be part of something bigger, but I had no idea the journey I would be taken on by the impact of this movie.

I was pregnant at the age of 16 and gave birth to my son at the age of 17, so I knew the emotions that young women in crisis go through. We each have our own story. My older daughter had an abortion at the age of 19 and I never realized until that moment the anguish and pain that she dealt with daily was due to the loss of her child. The movie constantly played in my head. I could not stop thinking about it.

Four days later, on April 19, I was faced with an emergency hysterectomy. On May 12 I had 20 blood clots go to my lungs and was not expected to live. At the moment the doctor asked me what they could do to make me comfortable. I knew this was it. I told him to tell my family I love them and to knock me out so

I didn't know what was happening. I closed my eyes and stood before Jesus with my head low, saying, "I have not been serving You as I should." I woke up in ICU and was told there was no medical reason for me to have survived, and with no heart or lung damage. I spent the next few months battling with more trials. Every month was something else. And with the constant replaying of *October Baby* going through my mind, I knew I was being led into ministry.

In October 2012 I was invited to attend the CareNet conference in Nashville, Tennessee. One of their guest speakers was Shari Rigby from the movie *October Baby*. As she began to tell her story I began to shake. The similarities in our stories were truly astonishing, from early life right through to when we both became pregnant with our second child while working for a law firm. I was married, but had no idea how I was going to be able to take care of another child, and I had just started working with the firm. I had to make a choice. I knew God but I did not have a relationship with Him as I do now. I knew that I was going to carry to term, but the choice could have been different if the love and support of my family were not there for me.

After hearing Shari speak I stood in line and waited to get her autograph and let her know the impact her life and her story had on me. She could feel me shaking and she stood up from the table and hugged me and said, "We are soul sisters." I wept that night for Shari. I wept for all the women that have been faced with this decision and the pain they felt after, when the choice was to terminate their pregnancy. Shari's story not only made me breathless but impacted me in a way that I felt comfortable leaving my corporate job and began working for the local crisis pregnancy center. I had been led into this ministry to help women facing these same decisions and choices. In June 2013 I was called to Tennessee to build a shelter for young women faced with these decisions. Shari inspired me and gave me the courage to follow the call that God had placed in my life, and Shari has been a significant part of this journey.

I began to follow Shari's ministry, "The Women in my World," and have established a friendship with her. My younger daughter and I had the pleasure of hearing her speak again exactly a year after we had met at the Tennessee Right to Life banquet in October 2013, and I witnessed the lives of those around her that she had touched. Not a dry eye in the room. Her strength and courage to share her pain, her story to help those that desperately needed to be freed from shame and guilt that is carried every day. To know that they are not alone, that God is there for Shari and there for every one of us. Shari offers hope to the brokenhearted. She is a true faithful servant of God, and I can say that I would not be where I am today and leading my ministry if it had not been for the movie *October Baby* and hearing Shari's testimony. She has given me strength and courage and remains a true inspiration to me. You are Wonder Woman, my sweet dear friend. Thank you.

Love you, girl. God bless you!

July 2013

Hi, Shari. I am a single mom with four children. I would like to request prayer. I have been through unbelievable hardships, but I know God has a plan for my life. I am very inspired by you. My divorce was finalized last year but it has been a three-year process. My faith in God has helped me through some of the worst times of my life. I was in an abusive relationship and I began to not see anything pretty about myself at all. It was a painful experience and I pray that some good will come out of it. Since the separation, I have signed with a modeling agency and have been able to meet and work with some wonderful people. I would love to be able to be involved in some faith-based films, and I pray that my involvement would bring glory to God and help other women. Please pray for me in my new journey that God would keep my children and I safe and help me to provide for them. Thank you so much for taking the time to read my email, and thank you in advance for praying for my children and I.

May 2014

I had an abortion as a sophomore in college, 13 years ago now, following a rape in a New Orleans bathroom. I pushed those memories away, I mean completely shut it down for close to 10-11 years. Sex, drinking excessively, cocaine, I did whatever I had to do to stop my brain from "going there."

About 3 years ago I finally got the nerve to call a local pregnancy center and join a Bible study, "Forgiven and Set Free." After a very rough several weeks with a few dear ladies, I finally processed my actions. Anger, grief, the works. I finally put a gender and a name to the only child I've ever conceived, and laid to rest her precious soul, entrusting her to her heavenly Father. I wasn't "ready" to watch *October Baby* when it first came out. It wasn't until earlier this year when I sat down, cued it up on Netflix, not sure exactly what to expect. I immediately connected with your character. That moment…with you sliding down the wall, sobbing…girl, I HAD that moment. I was sobbing too. I happened to be doing something in the kitchen as the credits rolled, and I was taken in as you shared so bravely with the world your story. I knew that moment you had seemed so raw, so real. I am thankful to you for your story and your role in the movie. Thank you so much.

April 2012

I'm a 1973 post-abortive mother who at the age of 19 aborted my son who would now be 41. When *October Baby* the movie came out I thought that I had been totally healed from the pain, shame and guilt of my abortion but really I hadn't. Even though I had shared about my abortion with a small group of women from my church from time to time I still felt I had never grieved the loss of my son.

When I heard about *October Baby* I felt like "This is a movie I have to see." It meant even more to me being that I have two daughters with October birthdays.

The major point of the movie that stood out to me and impacted my life deep was when you, Shari, read the note left on your desk that had the words written, "I forgive you" and you slid down the door. I could feel your pain so greatly and mine also and just sobbed along with you. I felt like my son had left me that note as well and I didn't even know about your own story, your abortion and what God had done for you through this movie. I thought this was just you acting your part and you did an awesome job.

When the movie was over a lady was sitting next to my sister in a different area of the theater asked her if she'd had an abortion. My sister answered no, I'm here to support my sister, as she knew I was grieving my son. The lady asked my sister if she could meet me and everything happened so fast as so many women in the theatre were very emotional. The lady came over and introduced herself and gave me a hug, told me Jesus loved me and handed me a card telling me to call the phone number if I needed any kind of post-abortion help. Through the movie and in the theater God was doing a work in the lives of many women there, including my own.

After seeing the movie on April 24, 2012, I attended the Crisis Pregnancy Center fundraising dinner event and made the commitment with the center director to become a peer counselor and started my training in May.

Not only did the movie move me to become a voice for the

voiceless and unborn, but my oldest daughter also made a commitment to become a peer counselor as well. In May of 2012, we both started our journey with the Crisis Pregnancy Center and attended the training session and have now been serving as volunteers with CPC for 2 years.

Through my journey of healing from my past abortion and viewing *October Baby*, the movie made a big impact in my family's life as well. As of Feb this year 2014, my son-in-law and my nephew are now male mentors for the Choices (Crisis) Pregnancy Center as well. This is now a family affair, a family of four being a voice for those who have no voice. To me all that I have gone through to get my breakthrough was ordained by the Lord and God used *October Baby* and you, Shari Rigby, to impact my life greatly. I thank you for your transparency.

Spring 2014

My story begins 28 years ago. I was 14 years old and as a result of being raped, I became pregnant. I was taken out of state to an abortion clinic to terminate the pregnancy. I was then hypnotized so I wouldn't remember the pregnancy or the abortion. I was told, something was "wrong" with me and I needed to have an "operation."

About 3 years ago, memories of the event began to surface. Mother's Day was tormenting although I have two beautiful, healthy children. Baby dedications at church were more than I could handle, and Sanctify of Life Sunday was a big "no." Although I considered myself pro-life, I had repressed so many feelings and emotions for so many years that I didn't understand why I was dealing with the emotions I was having. If you had asked me if I had an abortion, my answer would have been "no." It was that distant of a memory for me.

The first time I watched *October Baby*, I was actually

attending a post-abortive Bible study called "Forgiven and Set Free." I remember watching in awe as Cindy Hastings (played by Shari Rigby) grasped the piece of paper that said "I forgive you" and slid down that wall. I knew it was so much more than acting, as I felt the presence of God flood over my own life as healing saturated my soul. For the first time in a very long time, I cried. I really cried. The tears flowed freely as I received the love of my Savior as well as the assurance that my baby is in heaven with Jesus and is free and whole.

The memories of my abortion no longer torment me. I have watched *October Baby* 26 times to date and every time, I shed tears as I watch Shari being healed in that scene. I have shared with several women the power and impact of that movie as I have sat and held the hands of those who needed to receive forgiveness. God has truly used the movie *October Baby*, as well as the friendship of Shari, to remind me of His love and forgiveness on many occasions.

My heart is to see each woman affected by abortion, whether forced or by choice, healed…forgiven and set free!

I thank God for Shari Rigby…for her heart and her passion to reach hurting women. God puts special people in our lives for a reason and I am blessed to call Shari my friend.

14

Shine Like a Diamond

>—⊷—◦—⊷—◦

"Oh, how greatly I've been forgiven and how
grateful I am that my Savior didn't come for the
righteous but for the sinner...for me!"

SHARI RIGBY

This is really the beginning, a continuation of my story, with so
much more to come. I am so thankful you have made it to the
end of my book and to this part of my journey. Looking back
at my past, I realize God was preparing me for my future, and I
have been extremely blessed to experience so much redemption,
restoration, and hope. While it is a story of imperfection, it is also
a testament to how we are all beautifully flawed.

I originally began telling my story as a way to encourage
young teenage moms—girls just like me who had experienced
hardships in their lives but still wanted to be successful women.
My sassy bend was, "Don't let anyone tell you you can't do this or
you're not good enough." Young women need to know they are
loved and can achieve their dreams no matter how messy their
lives might look, despite whatever choices they have made. However, my audience began to grow as I too began to grow, and I felt

led to encourage *all* women, letting them know no matter what age you are, you can be a success.

As my journey continued and I rededicated my life to Christ, my *story* began to take on a new shape, one with even more substance. My marriage, my family, my involvement in church and women's ministry all impacted me, shaping my voice and growing my vision. I now wanted to grab ahold of each person I met and tell them, "You can be loved and cherished. You have a purpose. You are worthy, beautiful, unique and different all at the same time because you were purposefully created by a Savior that loves you!" Our Savior is a man who came to die for us, to leave His words of truth, to tell the story of a real leading man, an example for other men to follow, who treats women like the leading ladies they are.

I eventually came to a place where I wanted to stand on a mountaintop and scream these truths. Then the time finally came for me to have a mountain to stand on. My dreams were coming true; I had been cast in the movie *October Baby*. As I took this journey on-screen and digested the script, there it was, the line: "To be human is to be beautifully flawed." A beautiful statement of truth about life, about me, about thousands of others—not shame or condemnation but freedom and forgiveness. Right there, I could see myself as human, beautiful, and flawed, as well as forgiven, set free, and able to use my past story to encourage others.

Just as a roller coaster has many ups and downs, twists and turns, so has the pathway of my life. Even when it seemed like I was about to fly off the tracks, I was given another chance to get back on the straight and narrow, to make better choices and continue on with purpose. I began to identify myself as a *leading lady* to the Lord, and I'm so thankful He never gave up on me. Instead He continued to pursue me as a gentleman, allowing me to come to Him in my time, to eventually love Him with all my heart. He redeemed me and showed me what real love looks like.

As I end this book, I want you to know that no matter what has happened in your life, you can still get out of the boat, walk in freedom, and carry out the unique purpose you were created for. Once you have been redeemed, the restoration process begins. It will not be easy, but it is necessary in order to bring you to your full potential, to help you recognize who you really are and what you are capable of.

A diamond has to go through a refining process in order for it to become the beautiful gem that it is. What begins as simply carbon is put under intense heat and pressure before it eventually becomes a precious stone. The diamond still has flaws, both internal and external, but the flaws are what give each stone its uniqueness. It is then formed and polished, becoming the best it can possibly be in order to reach its greatest point of beauty. So it is the same with us, my friend, so shine brightly!

God is constantly changing us, molding us, and using our pasts to make beautiful presents. Despite everything I have been through, I have been given a chance to be a warrior for Christ, to serve others, and to move forward in God's plan. I encourage you to look at your life with hope, to know you too are beautiful and can move forward in freedom thanks to God's love and grace. You are worthy! You are special! He will use your flaws for His glory. He sees you as beautiful!

Blessings,
Shari

About the Authors

Shari Rigby made her start modeling and doing commercials. After moving to Los Angeles, she began a career in acting at an age when most actresses were retiring. Her most recent projects include, *The Summers Sisters* TV pilot, *Boonville Redemption* and *Wildflower*, releasing 2015, *Not Today*, which received seven awards, and *October Baby*, named one of the "Top 15 Impressive Box Office Performances of 2012" by CNN. Shari is currently working on creating faith-based film and television, Bible studies, and women's conferences.

Shari now speaks to thousands of people at churches and conferences, and she is a regular guest on radio and television programs—appearing on CBN, TBN, American Family Radio, Focus on the Family, K-Love Radio, and many more. She is founder of The Women in My World, a women's group focusing on identity, purpose, ministry, and living life in Hollywood. Shari is also a devoted mother to two boys, Donnie and Levi, and has been married to her husband, Matt, for seventeen years.

Claire Yorita Lee, a former recipient of the ABC/Disney Writing Fellowship and the FOX Diversity Writer's Initiative, Claire has worked on a number of TV shows and pilots, including NBC's *Medium*, where she sold a story. She wrote a short, "My Life Disoriented," funded by an ITVS grant, which premiered on PBS's *Independent Lens*. She wrote another short, "Engaged," which had its television debut on Sky Angel 2. She has a chapter in the recently published book, *Moms' Night Out and Other Things I Miss*, a devotional written for the film, *Moms' Night Out*."

Claire is currently working on her second teleplay for Discovery Family's *Transformers: Rescue Bots*, and is co-writing the film script for Kerri Pomarolli's book, *Guys Like Girls Named Jennie*. Claire lives in Southern California with her husband, Ed, and three children.

Acknowledgments

This is the one page that I couldn't wait to get to. I've envisioned many times in my life when I would get to say thank you to friends and family who have taken this life journey with me and have encouraged me to dream big, never give up, and reach for the stars.

Claire Lee, I could not have done this without you! From the moment we met and you said yes to taking on this endeavor with me, you have been the driving force to see us make it to the finish line. Without you, this project would still be in the baby stages. Thank you, friend, for pushing me, asking all the right questions, talking out my vision with me, and helping me shape my story. You are such a blessing in my life and I look forward to our next writing journey!

To my gift from God, my husband, Matt. You are truly the light in my life! You have been a constant. You are my hero. You have taught me how to say, "I'm sorry," and how to be a better person. I'm so thankful that you have loved me like I was as pure as snow from the moment you met me. I love you!

My sons, Donnie and Levi. You are the two greatest gifts a mother could have ever asked for. I am so blessed to be your mom. I know you will both achieve your dreams. You are both brilliant men of God.

Mom and Dad, thank you for always being there for me. I couldn't have made it through the many years of trials and tribulations without you both standing by my side. Thank you for helping me raise Donnie and giving him what he needed when I couldn't.

To my brother, Randy, and his wife, Stephanie, one of my longest and dearest friends. Thank you for all your love. We have shared so many good laughs and made memories that I will never forget. Ryan, Megan, and Lynzy, I love you and am so proud to be called your auntie.

My mother-in-law, Pam, for taking the time to help me bring *Beautifully Flawed* to life in the early stages. Your willingness to come alongside to help tell my story is a true testament of your love for me.

Jim and Pam, thank you for taking Donnie and me into your family and making us feel loved, wanted, and like we belonged right from the beginning.

James, Jodi, Jordin, PJ, Jessica, and Baby Ava, I love you all and am so thankful for all the years we have had together and the memories. Jodi, I'm so happy to see your eyes sparkle when you look at James.

To my dear friend and sister, Kris. Thank you for always being there for me. I will never forget the day we met, all the Heart we used to sing together and biscuits-and-gravy runs we made during high school. LRD will forever go down in my memories. Scott and kids, I love you all.

To my friend and manager, a man who has always believed in me, Joe Battaglia. Thank you for your love and kindness toward me. Your wisdom, pep talks, laughter, and support are truly gifts from God. LuAnn makes you even better! Now, go get a milkshake!

Pastor Mark Martin, thank you for sharing the message of grace with me so many years ago and for introducing me to Jesus.

Chaz Corzine, thank you for giving me a start and believing that I just might have it! Because you said yes, you gave way to starting my career.

John Kirby, from the day that I first walked into your studio I felt like a star. Thank you for being my friend and teacher. Guiding me through this journey called acting. You always make me better and help give me such a story to tell through a movie script.

Nathan Nesbitt, thank you for always encouraging me and taking care of my needs.

Stephanie Lanier, sweet friend and travel guru partner. Thank you for your friendship and your constant encouragement. Oh, and your amazing organizational skills.

The Erwin family. Thank you so much for giving me a voice to share my story with thousands of men and women all over the world. I'm so grateful to you all for giving me an opportunity to be a part of *October Baby*. Life changing!

Gary and Moira Sinise. Thank you for stepping out and seeing *October Baby*. Thank you for blessing me with your friendship and continued support. You are two of my heroes.

Susannah Hicks, prayer warrior and faithful friend. Thank you for your constant encouragement and prayers during my journey.

The Women in My World, I love you all! Each and every one of you has inspired me, made me a better woman, and loved me beyond my wildest dreams.

Kristi. Thank you for always telling me to go for it. I will never forget your constant faith in my dreams.

Anna Redmon, my sister from another mother. I love you and have found such inspiration in your words of wisdom. You inspire me! Of course, thank you for always picking out the perfect clothes for me.

Cecil Stokes. Friend, you are amazing! Thank you for always encouraging me and speaking truth into my life.

Rachel Hendrix, I am inspired by you. Thank you for loving me!

October Baby family: Colleen Trusler, Jason Burkey, cast and crew. I'm so blessed by our friendship and how the Lord brought us all together to tell a story that will forever impact a generation.

To Carlton Garborg, David Sluka, and the BroadStreet Publishing Group family. Thank you for coming alongside me to bring my story to life and getting it out to share with men and women around the world.

Ambassador Speakers Bureau, Gloria and team. Thank you for working around the clock to book me on speaking gig after speaking gig. I hope we get to do it again!

Jodi Breneman. Thank you for taking the time to hit the road with me. To be my prayer warrior and to hold my hand when I needed it.

Dream Center family, Matthew and Caroline Barnett, Ida, Tom Gehring, and all. Thank you for blessing me with your love and acceptance. I am so blessed to be part of the Dream Center and I love knowing that as a misfit, I am welcome!

The Polis family. Thank you for always helping with Levi and being his second family when we needed you.

Bill Reeves, WTA team. Thank you for always supporting me and constantly helping me grow as an actress, person, and storyteller.

Ben Howard and the Provident team. Thank you for your support and encouragement.

Pat Layton and Surrendering the Secret team. Thank you for your prayers and partnership with *October Baby*. Praise the Lord for your hearts to see men and women healed from past abortions.

Kerri Pomarolli. Thank you for being such a sweet friend. You helped me walk through all my needs in making the decision to move forward with my book. Thank you for introducing me to Claire! She has helped change my life.

JBird and Franklin Graham family. Thank you for giving me an opportunity to be a part of your ministry events. So blessed by every journey!

Melissa Skoff, thank you for your friendship and love.

Again, many, many thanks to you all! For everyone who has crossed my path, shared a season with me, or remained a friend for years, thank you for impacting my life.

Notes for quotes that start each chapter

Chapter 1
Some sources attribute this to Harriet Morgan, other say source is unknown.

Chapter 2
Lorna Luft, *Me and My Shadow: A Family Memoir* (New York, NY: Pocket Books, a division of Simon and Schuster, Inc., 1989), 166.

Chapter 3
Brandon Boyce, *Wicker Park* (Metro-Goldwyn-Mayer, MGM, released in the US in September 2004).

Chapter 4
Kurt Cobain interview, *Rolling Stones*, April 16, 1992.

Chapter 5
http://www.searchquotes.com/quotation/Don't_worry_girls,_one_day_you'll
_find_a_guy_who_ruins_your_lipstick,_not_your_mascara./367833/

http://boardofwisdom.com/togo/Quotes/ShowQuote?msgid=502443#
.VFAvlytdV9s. Anonymous.

Chapter 6
Markus Zusak, *The Book Thief* (New York, NY: Alfred F. Knopf, 2005).

Chapter 7
William Shakespeare, *A Midsummer Night's Dream*, Act 1, Scene 1 (Random House, Inc., 1980).

Chapter 8
http://boardofwisdom.com/togo/?viewid=1012&listowner=taciturn&start=53
1&m=1#.VFBDBytdV9s. Some attribute this to Marilyn Monroe.

Chapter 9
Francine Rivers, *Redeeming Love* (Colorado Springs, CO: Multnomah Books, 1997).

Chapter 10
C. S. Lewis, *Mere Christianity* (New York, NY: Macmillan, 1952), 163.

Chapter 11
C. S. Lewis, *Mere Christianity* (New York, NY: Macmillan, 1952), Preface.

Chapter 12
Jon Erwin, Teresa Preston, Andy Erwin and Cecil Stokes, Officer Mitchell, *October Baby* (Provident Films, Gravitas, released October 2011, re-released March 2012).